Mauzy's Kitchen Collectibles

Barbara and Jim Mauzy

4880 Lower Valley Road, Atglen, PA 19310 USA

Dedication

With hugs and kisses and lots of love to Sue Dibeler AKA Hazel AKA Haz. We appreciate all you do and who you are. We are in awe of your math skills while remaining vastly impressed with your people skills. Thanks for being y-o-u. Love Auntie Barbara, Jimmy Mike, and the Girls.

Published by Schiffer Publishing Ltd.
4880 Lower Valley Road
Atglen, PA 19310
Phone: (610) 593-1777; Fax: (610) 593-2002
E-mail: Info@schifferbooks.com

Designed by Mark David Bowyer
Type set in Kitchen Kapers II, Poster Bodoni BD/Souvenir Lt BT

ISBN: 0-7643-2107-2
Printed in China
1 2 3 4

For the largest selection of fine reference books on this and related subjects, please visit our web site at **www.schifferbooks.com**
We are always looking for people to write books on new and related subjects. If you have an idea for a book please contact us at the above address.

This book may be purchased from the publisher.
Include $3.95 for shipping.
Please try your bookstore first.
You may write for a free catalog.

In Europe, Schiffer books are distributed by
Bushwood Books
6 Marksbury Ave.
Kew Gardens
Surrey TW9 4JF England
Phone: 44 (0) 20 8392-8585; Fax: 44 (0) 20 8392-9876
E-mail: info@bushwoodbooks.co.uk
Free postage in the U.K., Europe; air mail at cost.

Contents

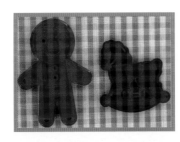

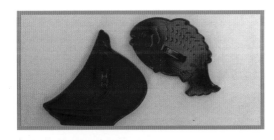

Acknowledgments

The most sincere thanks go to these collectors who opened their homes to us. Everyone was so helpful and fun to be with as we waded through this process. Mostly all of these collectors and friends need to be applauded for their undying patience as no one thought it would take years for us to utilize these pictures. Special thanks to Kim Boyer for providing many of the red-handled tools and gadgets.

JoAnn Baum
Kim A. Boyer
Almeda H. Brackbill
Tom Dibeler and Les Fawber / L.E. Fawber Antiques
David and Audrey Krzeminski /
    Good Shepherd Farms
Mr. and Mrs. Robert W. Lockerman
Sally and Herbie Loeb
Christine and Charles Olsen
Donna Panici
Ringer's 1840 Homestead
Brenda R. Smeltz
Jeff Snyder

 # Preface

Dear Readers:

The Complete Book of Kitchen Collecting was published in 1997 and with that came a new venture for us. We have been busy researching and writing about vintage kitchenware from the 1920s-1950s ever since.

In the midst of our work we got sidetracked by two things: Depression Glass and slide format images. Since 1996 a box of photographs sat under our desk ignored and forgotten. Between a lack of time due to other book projects and the realization that slide images worked better for book building we had abandoned these pictures. Then we took another look and all we could say was, "Wow!" We decided there was some really neat stuff in that box, we turned it into this book, and we hope you agree. Not only is there a vast assortment of kitchen collectibles, we were able to provide an interesting assortment of advertisements, catalogue information, and original packaging. Our wish is that as you turn the pages you validate our decision to put together another book on kitchen collectibles.

Thanks for your ongoing support of our work! We enjoy the enthusiastic responses we receive and welcome your comments.

Now for your help: We would like to compile pictures of kitchens that have vintage wares on display. If you are willing to submit pictures for possible use in a future book we will accept prints WITH negatives or slides (our first choice!) Please mail them to us along with all of your contact information and notes about your kitchen and collection.

Barbara and Jim Mauzy
P.O. Box 207
Akron, PA 17501

The quality of the pictures is even more important than the subject matter, and nothing will be returned.

Back in the 1990s Barbara spent some time photographing kitchens and what follows are some examples of what you can do with the kinds of items that are pictured in this book. As these images were taken in our early years of photography they are not quite up to standard. Hopefully the wonderful items in these pictures more than compensate for Barbara's amateur efforts.

An interesting arrangement of kitchen-related advertising shows that done right "more can be better." *Courtesy of Tom Dibeler and Les Fawber.*

Additional vintage packages are displayed in an old cupboard. *Courtesy of Tom Dibeler and Les Fawber.*

Wooden spoons and beaters are displayed among pitchers and bowls in rarely seen colors. *Courtesy of Tom Dibeler and Les Fawber.*

Wooden tools from the 1800s fill an old wooden
bowl. *Courtesy of Ringer's 1840 Homestead.*

An old cupboard and painted firkins
frame the beauty of white ironstone.
Courtesy of Ringer's 1840 Homestead.

Colors abound in a room bursting with old color. *Courtesy of Ringer's 1840 Homestead.*

Jade-ite mugs create part of the border in a green and white kitchen devoted to the beauty of Fire-King. *Courtesy of Jeff Snyder.*

An interesting array of Clover Farm collectibles is arranged together. *Courtesy of David and Audrey Krzeminski / Good Shepherd Farms.*

Blue in the old paint, pottery, and homespun fabric strike a lovely balance with white ironstone. *Courtesy of David and Audrey Krzeminski / Good Shepherd Farms.*

Lard cans are hung from a drying rack above a kitchen window. *Courtesy of Sally and Herbie Loeb.*

Vivid wallpaper adds color and excitement to an interesting mix of collectibles. *Courtesy of Sally and Herbie Loeb.*

Fiesta colors spill through this kitchen. Of particular interest are the fruit embellishments on the bottom of the shade. *Courtesy of Brenda R. Smeltz.*

Transparent green and jade-ite green fill a vintage Hoosier-type kitchen cabinet. *Courtesy of JoAnn Baum.*

11

Collecting and decorating with a theme, such as tomatoes shown here, creates a truly unique kitchen. *Courtesy of Mr. and Mrs. Robert W. Lockerman.*

Green-handled kitchen tools look right at home on a counter filled with vintage jade-ite. *Courtesy of JoAnn Baum.*

The kitchen phone is almost totally camouflaged among a wall of old needlework and vintage kitchen tools hung on pegs. *Courtesy of Christine and Charles Olsen.*

Every inch is utilized to maximize an interesting and colorful display. *Courtesy of Mr. and Mrs. Robert W. Lockerman.*

Although the colors are muted in this image, one can still appreciate the beauty of grouping many single-colored wooden handles together in large number. *Courtesy of Donna Panici.*

Simple displays offer beauty, too. Here are pottery candy containers from the 1920s paired with old tin. *Courtesy of Almeda H. Brackbill.*

13

Every nook of space is utilized. Here a corner under the kitchen cupboards showcases green-handled tools from the late 1920s and 1930s with tin and wood. *Courtesy of Christine and Charles Olsen.*

Red and green handles add color to a display of old tin. *Courtesy of Christine and Charles Olsen.*

Packaging, both large and small, in metal, cardboard, and glass showcase American products from previous decades. *Courtesy of Christine and Charles Olsen.*

14

About the Book and the Prices

This book is designed to illustrate the plethora of kitchen collectibles from the 1920s-1950s. Although not fully inclusive, these pages offer a showcase of vintage tools and more that are lovely to see, easy to use, and interesting to collect.

We have done everything possible to provide accurate prices. We have monitored the Internet, auctions, and trade papers, gone to shows, and consulted with collectors and dealers. We bring to this effort our years of buying, selling, and collecting kitchen collectibles. If you are familiar with our other books and our website (www.TPTT.net) you know this is a favorite subject of ours. Values vary immensely according to the condition of the piece, the location of the market, and the overall quality of the design and manufacture. Condition is always of paramount importance when assign-

ing a value. The prices shown in this reference are for individual items that are in mint condition, but not packaged. Prices in the Midwest differ from those in the West or East, and those at specialty shows will vary from those at general shows. And, of course, being at the right place at the right time can make all the difference.

All of these factors make it impossible to create an absolutely accurate price list, but we can offer a guide. The values shown in this reference reflect what one could realistically expect to pay but ultimately the seller and the buyer determine values as they agree upon a price.

Neither the authors nor the publisher are responsible for any outcomes resulting from this reference.

Beaters and Mechanical Whips

The earliest beaters were made totally of metal; wooden handles are largely from the twentieth century and colors were introduced in 1927. The beaters pictured in this 1938 article show an assortment that might have been in a kitchen from this era. Just as today, women did not randomly replace kitchen tools and their quality allowed decades of efficient, effective use.

The text of this article succinctly says it all: "There are many small items that encourage our best efforts. For instance, take beaters. Some really beat eggs while others beat your spirits. You can't judge them by looks, so try them before you buy one." The same holds true today. Whether a purchase is being made for decorative purposes or for actual use when cooking and baking, the blades need to spin smoothly.

The Country Home magazine, January 1938.

There was no copyright date for *How to make all kinds of good things to eat – with WESSON OIL,* a cookbook by and for Wesson Oil. A beater is prominently positioned in a scene from the late 1920s or early 1930s.

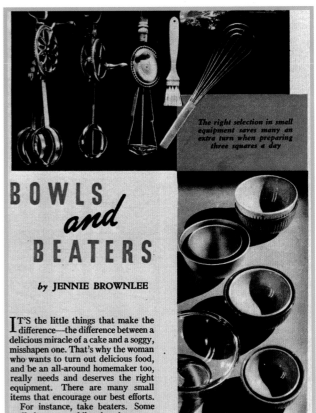

The right selection in small equipment saves many an extra turn when preparing three squares a day

BOWLS *and* BEATERS

by JENNIE BROWNLEE

IT'S the little things that make the difference—the difference between a delicious miracle of a cake and a soggy, misshapen one. That's why the woman who wants to turn out delicious food, and be an all-around homemaker too, really needs and deserves the right equipment. There are many small items that encourage our best efforts.

For instance, take beaters. Some really beat eggs while others beat your spirits. You can't judge them by looks, so try them before you buy one. First, the handles, on the top and wheel, should be comfortable for you to hold. Hold the beater in the beating position —not in the air—and turn the handle. If your hand moves in a fairly large circle, the job will seem less tiresome. Thin blades—eight of them—give the greatest volume and finest texture. You'll find a beater lasts longer if the cogs on the wheels and shafts are well-made and fitted together smoothly.

A pastry brush to grease your pans or spread butter smoothly on the rolls you're making will bring you through the process clean and neat.

A rubber paddle, a newcomer to

can be beautiful and good at the same time, but remember the most useful bowls have a small base and slightly curved and sloping sides. A beater does its best work in these small-bottomed bowls—and the small quantity that is the beginning of many a recipe isn't lost in the mixing.

The angel food experts who use a wire whip for beating egg whites will want a wide shallow bowl, in which long high strokes are possible. That means more air in the batter and more volume in the cake. Light bowls or heavy ones—both have their advantages. Those of aluminum and enamel

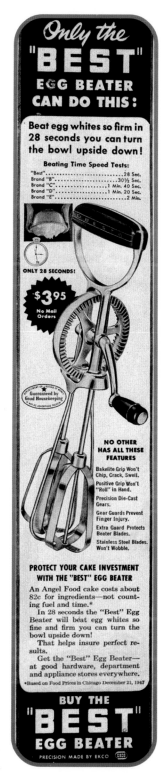

Bakelite handles were used primarily in the 1930s and 1940s and after World War II plastic was considered the modern material. A beater that would now sell for about $12-$15 was originally $3.95.

Beaters are a favorite with today's collectors. In fact, there are many collectors of beaters alone. Value is determined by two factors: condition and uniqueness of design.

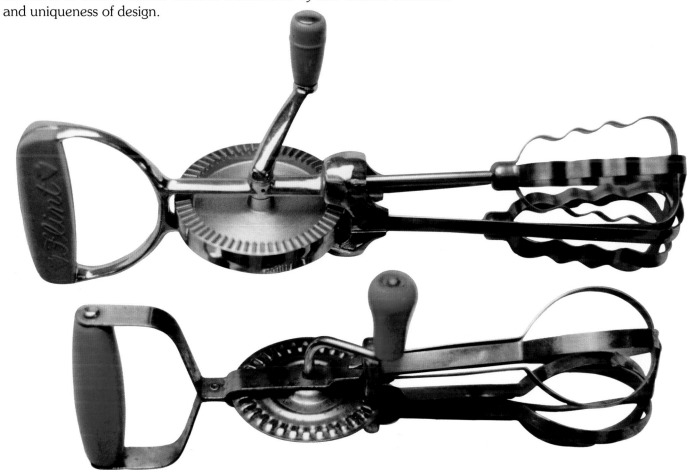

These are more traditional beater designs, although the plastic-handled Flint beater has unusual ridges that were supposed to enhance the efficiency and effectiveness of this tool. Made by EKCO, the 11.75" long plastic-handled tool with stainless steel beaters will be difficult to find. The 10.25" long wooden-handled beater is simply marked "STAINLESS" with no manufacturing information of any kind. Plastic, Circa early 1950s; wood, Circa 1930s. $18 each.

Ladies' Home Journal, June 1948.

Yellow is the primary kitchen color of the 1950s but this 11" long beater marked "THE TAPLIN MFG. CO. NEW BRITIAN CONN. PAT NO 1518285 MADE IN U.S.A." would have been a part of a brightly colored pre-WWII kitchen. The patent dates from 1924 and 1937 are for the mechanism as handle designs and colors were not protected with patents. Circa late 1930s-early 1940s. $12.

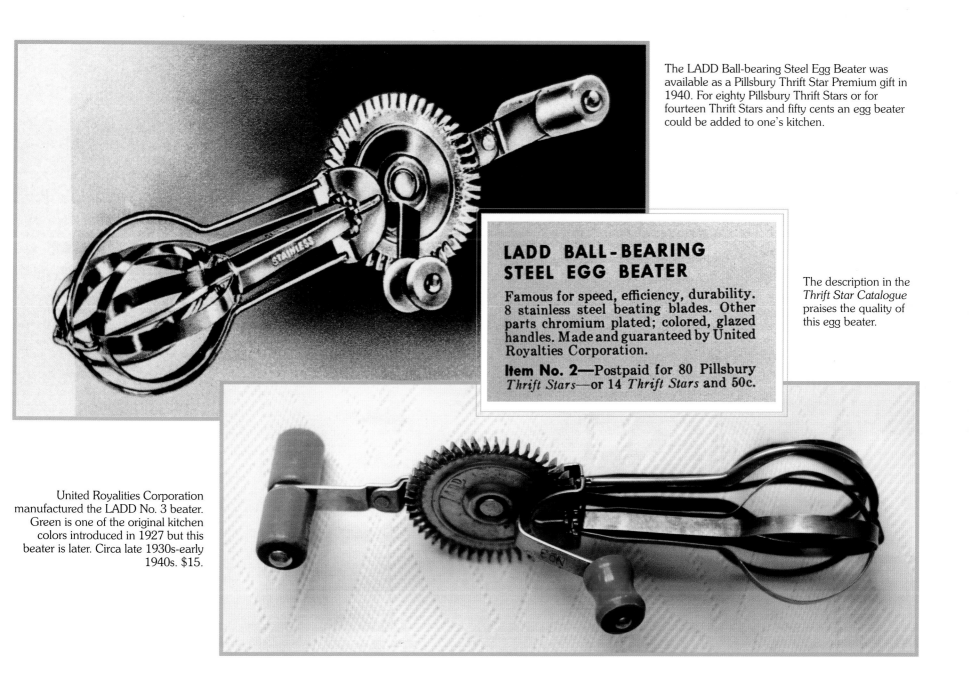

The LADD Ball-bearing Steel Egg Beater was available as a Pillsbury Thrift Star Premium gift in 1940. For eighty Pillsbury Thrift Stars or for fourteen Thrift Stars and fifty cents an egg beater could be added to one's kitchen.

LADD BALL-BEARING STEEL EGG BEATER

Famous for speed, efficiency, durability. 8 stainless steel beating blades. Other parts chromium plated; colored, glazed handles. Made and guaranteed by United Royalties Corporation.

Item No. 2—Postpaid for 80 Pillsbury *Thrift Stars*—or 14 *Thrift Stars* and 50c.

The description in the *Thrift Star Catalogue* praises the quality of this egg beater.

United Royalities Corporation manufactured the LADD No. 3 beater. Green is one of the original kitchen colors introduced in 1927 but this beater is later. Circa late 1930s-early 1940s. $15.

A & J manufactured this 13.5" long beater marked "A & J MADE IN U.S.A. PAT. OCT. 9-1923." The patent date is only for the mechanism; green handles weren't introduced until 1927. Circa 1930s. $18.

No patent information is on a 10.75" long red-handled A & J beater with the same mechanism as the previous beater. This is marked "EKCO A & J U.S.A." Circa 1930s. $18.

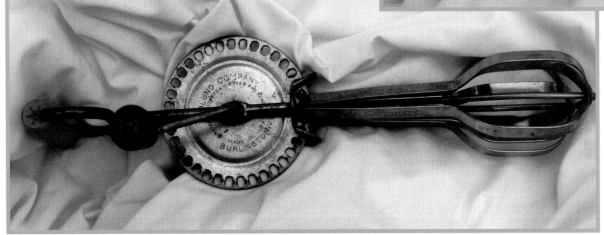

Edlund Company manufactured this 12.5" long wooden-handled beater that is marked "EDLUND COMPANY MADE IN U.S.A. BURLINGTON, VT. PATENT NO. 1789224 – OTHER PAT. PEND." The patent, which is only for the mechanism, is from 1930. Circa 1930s. $18.

Edlund Company used the mechanism shown on the previous beater with Bakelite handles. 11.75" in length, the manufacturer's marking is identical to that of their wooden-handled beater, "EDLUND COMPANY MADE IN U.S.A. BURLINGTON, VT. PATENT NO. 1789224 – OTHER PAT. PEND." The patent, which is only for the mechanism, is from 1930. Circa 1930s-early 1940s. $30.

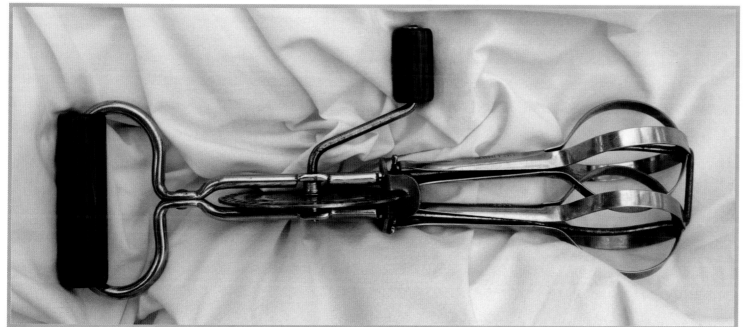

This angle better shows the ridged details of the Bakelite handles of the Edlund beater that is incredibly similar to Androck "Bullet" handles.

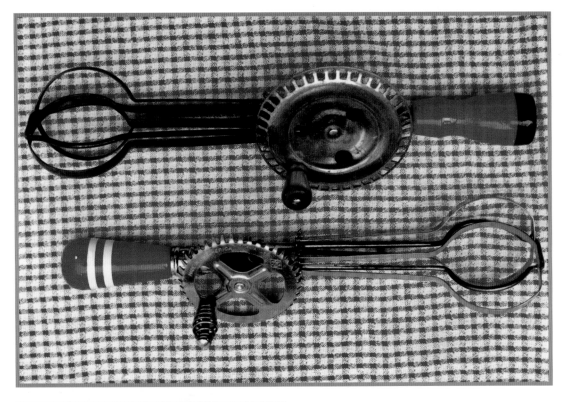

Introduced in 1927, red continues to be a favorite color with collectors. Shown are wooden-handled beaters by two different companies. The 10.75" long beater with white stripes is marked "A & J PAT OCT. 9-1923 MADE IN U.S. AMERICA." The 11.5" long beater is marked "WB" over another "W" and is also American-made. Circa 1930s. $18 each.

Looking much like a beater, the mechanism of this tool makes it a whip. This 11.25" long wooden-handled gadget is marked "SUPERSPEED A & J MADE IN U.S. AMERICA SPINNIT CREAM AND EGG WHIP." Circa 1930s. $35.

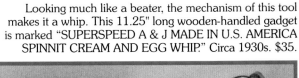

Shown is the manufacturer's information on the mechanism.

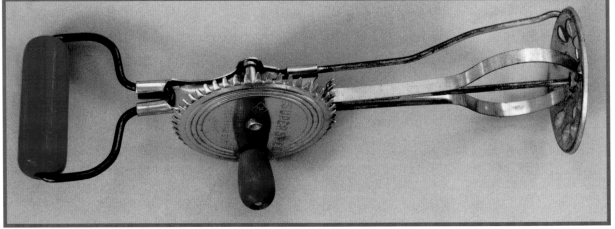

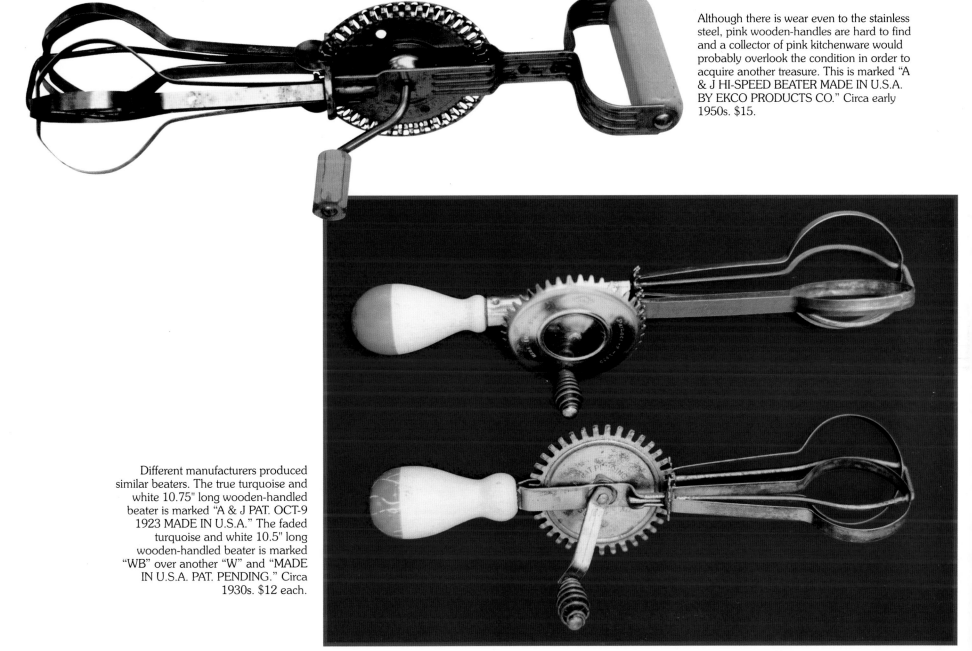

Although there is wear even to the stainless steel, pink wooden-handles are hard to find and a collector of pink kitchenware would probably overlook the condition in order to acquire another treasure. This is marked "A & J HI-SPEED BEATER MADE IN U.S.A. BY EKCO PRODUCTS CO." Circa early 1950s. $15.

Different manufacturers produced similar beaters. The true turquoise and white 10.75" long wooden-handled beater is marked "A & J PAT. OCT-9 1923 MADE IN U.S.A." The faded turquoise and white 10.5" long wooden-handled beater is marked "WB" over another "W" and "MADE IN U.S.A. PAT. PENDING." Circa 1930s. $12 each.

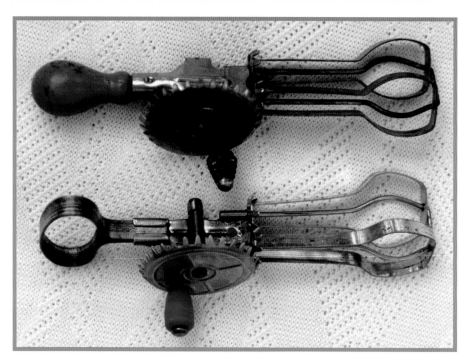

Manufacturers created an assortment of children's kitchen tools. The 5.5" red-handled beater is marked "Betty Taplin Beater" and the 5.75" long green-handled beater is marked "A & J MADE IN U.S. AMERICA PAT OCT. 9-1923." Value is largely determined by the condition of the mechanism; the blades need to rotate smoothly. Circa 1930s. $20 each.

The official name of these blue-handled tools is "Batter Beater." Gadgets with blue handles are difficult to find, particularly in this condition. Marked "A & J MADE IN UNITED STATES OF AMERICA BATTER BEATER Curved to fit the Bowl" these are identical except for the handle design. Circa 1930s. $18 each.

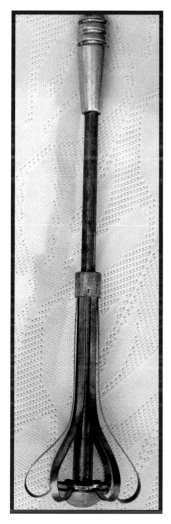

This 12.25" long rotating whip/beater is one of the most unique items in this section. It is marked "BOUN-C-BEATER PAT. PEND" on the base. Circa 1930s. $30.

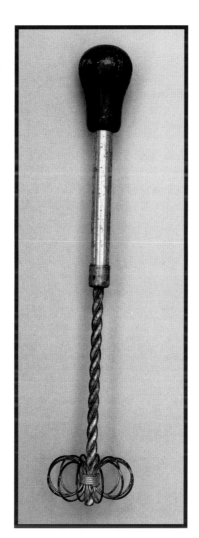

One-handed beaters and whips are very popular with collectors, and a blue handle adds to this gadget's appeal. This is almost 9.5" long and is marked "GERMANY BRITISH ZONE STEELCRAFT." Circa late 1940s. $25.

EKCO's 10.5" long wooden-handled egg beater is one of the most commonly-found turquoise-handled kitchen tools. Circa 1950s. $14.

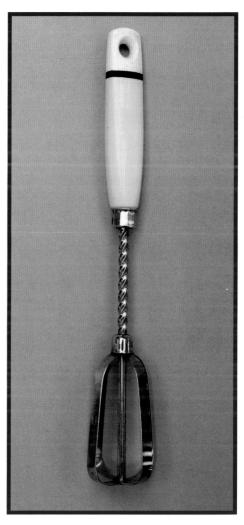

Marked "EKCO USA" this three-colored wooden-handled beater is 10.5" long. Circa 1950s. $15.

The same companies that produced hand-held beaters and whips also produced beaters with metal splash guards for use with measuring cups. Clear and transparent glass measuring cups are the most common, but an assortment of colors can be found in vintage glassware. Measuring cups can also be found in aluminum, but usually in used or worn condition with a lower value than the examples that follow.

It is not recommended that one purchase beater tops and bases separately as the correct fit is more than simply the diameter of the splash guard matching the diameter of the rim of the base. It is impossible to know if the beater and base create an appropriate match until the two are paired and the beater mechanism is rotated. Often beaters that seem to fit size-wise will not allow the beaters to operate.

11.5" tall, an A & J beater top is paired with a four-cup base marked "D & B." The top is marked "A & J PAT. OCT. 9-1923 MADE IN U.S.A." The transparent green base is embossed with pints, cups, and ounces. Circa late 1920s-early 1930s. $85.

The four-cup measure and beater top are both marked with A & J manufacturing information. The base of the measure has the following information molded into the glass: "A & J PATENT APPLIED FOR." The beater is marked "PAT. OCT. 9-1923 MADE IN U.S.A." Overall this is 12.5" tall. Circa late 1920s-early 1930s. $85.

This is the marking on the bottom of the four-cup measure.

Mechanical whips are difficult to find. Two 5" tall examples are presented with clear bases, but bases are found in a variety of opaque glass colors. Neither of these whips have any manufacturing information. Circa late 1930s-early 1940s. $60 each.

Bowls

There are scores of glass mixing bowls and mixing bowls sets made by an assortment of glass manufacturers. Shown are a few examples that barely do justice to this popular area of collecting. For a greater representation of vintage kitchen glassware *see Mauzy's Kitchen Glass.*

Anchor Hocking produced a line of Non-Splash bowls in the 1950s. Most of these were in sets of four, but a few individual bowls were manufactured for brief periods of time. This 7.5" diameter, 4.75" deep bowl is decorated with a Fred Press motif. The lid transforms the bowl into an ice bucket. Circa 1950s. $15 in worn condition as shown, $30 in pristine condition.

Rainbow bowls are part of Anchor Hocking's Fire-King line of oven proof glass. They are 9", 8", 7", and 6" in diameter and feature four different fired-on colors. Circa 1950s. Brown, $20; blue and yellow, $30 each; pink, $65.

Hazel-Atlas produced mixing bowls in a variety of transparent colors in a design that allowed them to stack or nest together minimizing the cabinet space needed to store them. This complete set of six bowls have diameters ranging from 10.75"-5.75" in one inch increments. Circa late 1920s-1930s. $250 for the set of six.

The shape of the bowls is more easily seen in this view.

Bread Boxes

Bread boxes are more popular than ever and no longer remain confined to the kitchen. Collectors and decorators have acknowledged their practicality as well as their beauty as one can store all kinds of treasures inside a bread box. They look great singly, grouped with matching tin ware, or stacked.

Bread boxes with drop down doors are more difficult to find and therefore of a higher value than those that have a removable or hinged lid. Most have matching tin ware including match safes, trash cans, sifters, and more.

Condition is very important both on the outside and inside. Collectors want items that remain lovely to look at while having little or no rust inside.

Polka dots add to the appeal of a bread box that has no manufacturing information but is known to be a NESCO (National Enameling and Stamping Company) item. An advertisement showing this motif is pictured in the "Canisters" section along with the matching canisters. Circa early 1940s. $35.

Flowers continue to be a popular theme in kitchenware. Although this has no manufacturer's marking, the matching and marked PARMECO (Parker Metal Decorating Company) canisters are shown in the "Canisters" section. There is an assortment of matching items with this spray of red roses to be collected. Circa 1930s-early 1940s. $35.

Manufacturers often "borrowed" ideas from one another, and when a design became popular the consumer had the ability to chose from an assortment of variations. NC Colorware created this bread box. Circa 1930s-early 1940s. $35.

This Deco Ware bread box originally sold for $1.89. There are canisters and other items with this simple leaf design. Circa late 1940s. $25.

The design of this bread box is the least commonly-seen variety. A plastic knob on top is gripped to pull up a metal drawer inside that is sized (5" x 5" x 10" tall) to hold a single loaf of bread. Circa 1930s. $75.

Roosters have been a favorite kitchen theme for several decades, and this crowing fellow was hand painted on many Ransburg items. Circa late 1940s-early 1950s. $35.

Bread boxes with double doors are among the favorite with today's collectors. The Deco Ware apple design can be found with white, cream, or yellow backgrounds. This is marked "CONTAINER PAT. APPL'D FOR MADE IN U.S.A." Circa 1930s. $60.

Nothing says "Depression Era" like the cream and green colors of this bread box. There is no manufacturer's information on this very popular container. Circa late 1920s and early 1930s. $75.

It is not uncommon to find an original sticker on Ransburg items; the glue must have created an unusually strong bond.

Harper J. Ransburg Company, Inc. created a huge assortment of metal kitchenware with hand painted embellishments. A 1953 advertisement in *Better Homes and Gardens* indicates there are "22 useful items...everything you need to create harmony and convenience throughout the kitchen."

"Kitchen Bouquet" is shown on a Ransburg bread box that has a plethora of matching kitchen items. Circa late 1940s-early 1950s. $35.

Give your kitchen that colorful Ransburg touch

Add new color and beauty to your kitchen with sparkling, hand-painted, colorful, Ransburg accessories. Every piece is free-hand painted, yet matches all others. Choose from 22 useful items—you'll find everything you need to create harmony and convenience throughout the room.

The clean, slick finish makes cleaning easy, upkeep effortless. Pattern and background are refrigerator type enamel, baked on sturdy steel for lasting loveliness.

RANSBURG
Originals
HAND PAINTED

Ask for Ransburg "Kitchen Bouquet" in ebony, red, white, yellow or gray. Buy a piece or so at a time, anytime you like—you'll love its matched set smartness. You can buy the entire matched set for much less than the cost of redecorating your kitchen—or you can start with the 4-piece canister set for about $5 and build your set a few pieces at a time. Write for the names of hardware and department stores near you featuring Ransburg originals.

Guaranteed by Good Housekeeping

HARPER J. RANSBURG CO., INC
Barth and Sanders Streets
Indianapolis 7, Indiana
Also available in Canada

Add dash and drama to your bath and powder rooms, too with Ransburg "Bath Bouquet." Available in burgundy, white, pink, yellow, blue and black.

33

Cake Carriers and Cake Savers

Cake carriers have some kind of system to lock the lid and base securely together allowing one to safely transport dessert. Cake savers are simply a cover and base that keep one's baked goods fresh. The metalware companies that produced cake carriers and cake savers are the same companies that created the bread boxes, canisters, and other metal products seen in vintage kitchens.

Condition and motif are critical factors when assessing value as most cake carriers are purchased with use in mind. Collectors want the inside to be as new-looking as the outside.

What follows is an interesting cross-section of metal cake carriers and a single cake saver. For a greater representation of cake carriers and savers see *Mauzy's Cake Plates.*

Deco Ware's pleasing floral motif decorated a cake carrier whose lid locks to the base with three metal clasps. Circa late 1940s-early 1950s. $35.

The carrying handle unhooks to open a cake carrier that has no manufacturing information. Circa 1930s. $30.

As the twentieth century progressed portion sizes, plates, and other kitchen items increased in size. This example is one of the largest and most recent pictured at 14.5" in diameter. West Bend created square and round cake carriers in copper and silver-tone. Circa 1950s. $30.

Red kitchenware has been popular since its introduction in 1927. A glass knob tops a cake carrier with a handle that clips the top and base together. "THIS SIDE UP" is embossed on the otherwise unmarked base. Circa 1930s. $35.

Although unmarked, this is thought to be a Peoria product. This cake and pie carrier features a narrow pie-sized compartment on top of a more generous cake-sized compartment. Circa 1950s. $25.

Deco Ware's apple design is found on a huge assortment of kitchenware including a cake saver. As the lid does not lock into the bottom one cannot accurately refer to this as a cake carrier. Circa 1930s. $35.

Is it Moxie or is it Maggie? Seems one of our Westies has been immortalized in a barbecue scene on a pie and cake carrier that has no manufacturer's information. Circa 1950s. $65.

Canisters

No kitchen item is as versatile as a set of canisters. Whether glass, metal, or plastic homemakers past and present often have more than one set and they may not be relegated to just the kitchen. Glass canisters are pictured in great detail in *Mauzy's Kitchen Glass.* This section will feature metal and plastic canisters from the 1930s-1950s.

Excellent condition of the inside and out is paramount for canisters to have the values shown here.

Garden themes are very popular and this set has many matching items. Circa 1930s-early 1940s. $12 each, $50 for a set of four.

This is one of the most popular designs by Deco Ware, and an assortment of companion pieces is available. Circa 1930s-early 1940s. $12 each, $50 for a set of four.

As the popularity of metal canisters continued some sets became available with five pieces. This set was available as a Pillsbury Thrift Star Premium with ninety stars or fifty-seven stars and twenty-five cents in 1940.

Two of the four canisters in a set by PARMECO (Parker Metal Decorating Company) are pictured. Bold sprays of roses add bursts of color to any kitchen. Circa 1930s-early 1940s. $12 each, $50 for a set of four.

Although there is no manufacturer's information on this canister set, an advertisement that follows identifies this as a NESCO item. Polka dots continue to be a favorite theme in kitchen décor. Circa early 1940s. $12 each, $50 for a set of four.

Featured as an exciting new ensemble in the March 1941 issue of *The American Home*, NESCO's canisters are shown with everything from a matching table cover to shakers.

KREAMER canisters feature a patent date from 1870, 102704. Bakelite handles make them much more recent than that and probably from the early 1940s. One must assume the canister design itself is protected with the early patent. Circa early 1940s. $15 each, $65 for a set of four.

Fruit are found in blue, red, and green in a design that is not particularly popular with today's collectors even though matching items are available. There is no manufacturing information on these canisters. Circa 1930s. $6 each, $25 for a set of four.

The use of flowers as a decorating theme continued into the middle of the Twentieth Century as seen on NESCO canisters that have a 1951 copyright date. Many matching accessories were produced. Circa 1951. $12 each, $50 for a set of four.

In 1951, Harper J. Ransburg Company, Inc. offered twenty-six matching kitchen items with hand painted embellishments. By 1953 Ransburg lines were reduced to twenty-two pieces. Either four items were too expensive to produce or there was not enough consumer demand to justify their production. The "six lively, lovely background colors" are shown in this advertisement found in the November 1951 *Better Homes and Gardens*.

"Kitchen Bouquet" is shown on Ransburg canisters that have a plethora of matching kitchen items. Circa late 1940s-early 1950s. $12 each, $50 for a set of four.

Roosters have been a favorite kitchen theme for several decades, and these proud-looking fellows were hand painted on many Ransburg items. Circa late 1940s-early 1950s. $12 each, $50 for a set of four.

The use of copper and aluminum for kitchen items is signature 1950s. The offer shown here was available in 1956 until June 30, 1957.

Plastic is another fifties material as utilized in pink and gray canisters in *Ladies' Home Journal* in February 1957.

There is no manufacturer's information on this set of plastic canisters. Plastic was a less-than-perfect material for canisters. Colors faded in bright sunlight and hard plastic was prone to cracking. Circa 1950s. $7 each, $30 for a set of four.

Chopper Jars

There are several features to consider prior to purchasing a chopper jar. The glass needs to be free from damage or cloudiness and a wooden disk (the shock absorber!) should be included. Test the mechanism: after a depression the handle should spring back without a great deal of wobbling.

The March 1941 issue of *The American Home* exults the usefulness of "Quick and easy" kitchen tools, and a Federal Tool Corporation chopping jar is praised for saving the chef's eyes when chopping onions.

Check the Grinder section for more examples.

Nine tools are recommended in the March 1941 issue of *The American Home.*

On rare occasions one can find a colored glass base. These are of much higher value than the examples that follow. The knobs and metal lids were made in a variety of colors, red being the most common. Knob materials include wood, Bakelite, and plastic.

Overall this is 10.25" tall. The glass base was manufactured by Hazel-Atlas and shows cups in 1/4-cup and 1/3-cup increments and ounces in 2-ounce increments. Circa early 1940s. $15.

Hazel-Atlas produced the 1-2/3 cup base for this 13" tall chopper jar. Circa early 1940s. $15.

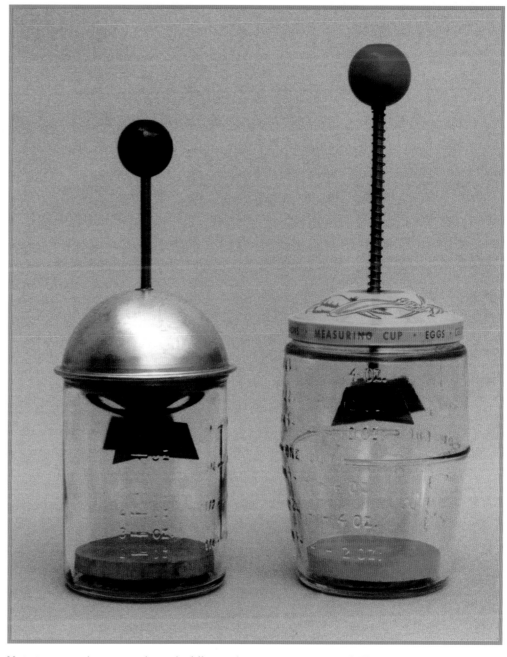

Variations on a theme, two distinctly different chopper jars are pictured. The jar with the black knob has "DISPENSERS, INC. LOS ANGELES - NEW YORK" embossed on the bottom of the base. The jar with the red knob has "SMALL VEGETABLES NUT MEATS ONIONS MEASURING CUP CELERY LIVER PARSLEY" encircling the rim of the lid. Circa early 1940s. $15 each.

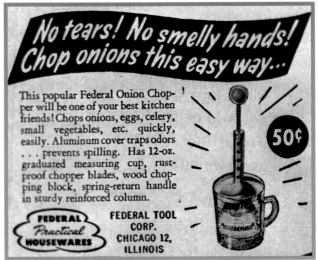

The Federal Onion Chopper was a mere fifty cents in 1948 as advertised in the June issue of *Ladies' Home Journal.*

Anchor Hocking made the "Automatic FOOD CHOPPER and MEASURING CUP" base with increments for ounces and quarter-cups shown in red. Pink handles are rare, and the Hazel-Atlas jar on the right is the newest one pictured. It has a twelve ounce capacity and increments embossed in the glass. Blue knob, Circa early 1940s. Pink knob and handle, Circa mid-1950s. $15 each.

Federal Tool Corporation offered this Nut Meat Chopper for only twenty-five cents in the March 1941 issue of *Ladies' Home Journal.*

One rarely hears the term "nut meat" today; we simply say "nut" or "nuts." A "Nut Meat Chopper" is designed to chop nuts. For either sixty cents or a dollar, depending on color versus chrome, one could own a Nut Meat Chopper as advertised in the November 1936 issue of *The American Home.*

The glass for the base of the Androck Uniform Nutmeat Chopper was manufactured by Hazel-Atlas. This is 6.25" tall. Circa 1940s. $18.

Choppers

Manual choppers have two basic designs: stationary blades and moveable blades. Among the stationary blades there are several configurations: one blade, multiple parallel blades, and multiple intersecting blades.

Excellent condition of the handles and the metal is imperative to a collector who intends to utilize this handy tool.

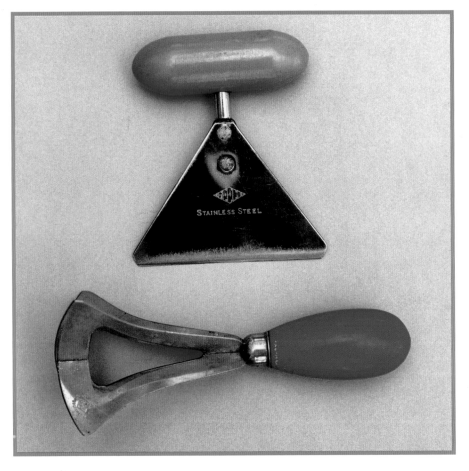

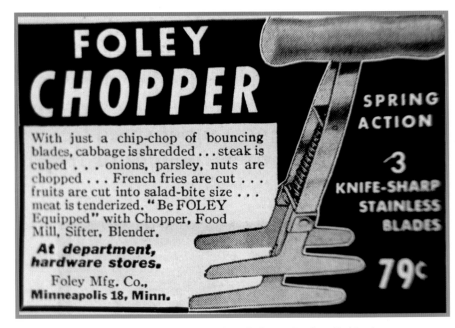

Foley choppers are among the most popular of all wooden-handled kitchen tools with collectors who know they need to be "FOLEY Equipped." This advertisement is from the June 1948 *Ladies' Home Journal.*

The blue-handled chopper is marked "SEECO STAINLESS STEEL" and is 4" tall with a 3" wooden handle. The 6" red-handled chopper is marked "A & J MADE IN UNITED STATES OF AMERICA." The plainness of the red handle suppresses its value. Circa 1930s. Blue, $14; red, $10.

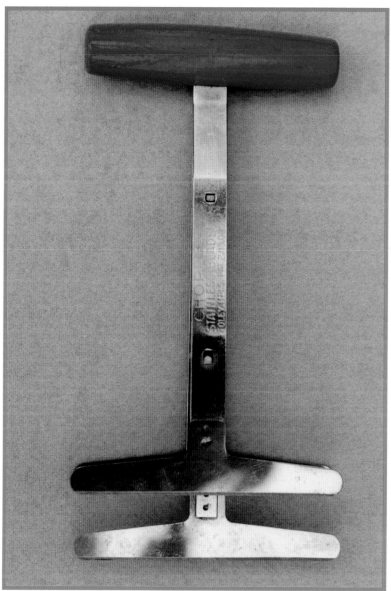

Foley choppers were made in red, green, black, turquoise, and yellow. They are 7.5" long with a 3.5" long wooden handle and include patent number 2,113,085 from 1938. They are also marked "CHOPPER STAINLESS BLADES FOLEY, MPLS." Circa 1938-early 1950s. $12 each.

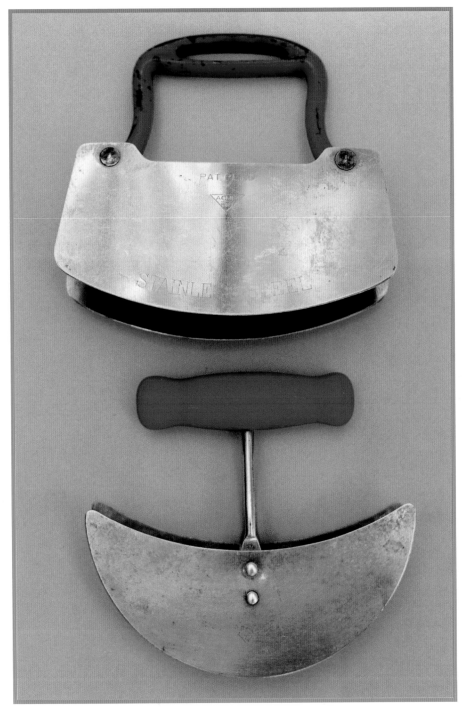

This 3.75" chopper with a large wooden knob is quite rare. Even though there is some chipping in the green paint the uniqueness of the design sustains its value. Circa 1930s. $20.

ACME manufactured both of these 5.5" red-handled choppers with double blades. The all-metal chopper is marked "ACME MGM CO. PAT. PEND. STAINLESS STEEL" and the wooden-handled chopper is marked "ACME MGM CO. MADE IN U.S.A." Circa 1930s. Metal handle, $15; wood handle, $20.

Cleaning Tools

The unfortunate part of cooking and baking is the inevitable clean up. Some interesting tools were created to ease the housewife's burden with this virtually incessant task. As cleaning tools were used, few have survived. Typically once they were worn out they would be discarded, therefore finding cleaning tools in excellent condition will be difficult.

The majority of the items shown in this section are brushes: long ones, thin ones, wide ones, all kinds for assisting in keeping Mother's kitchen tidy.

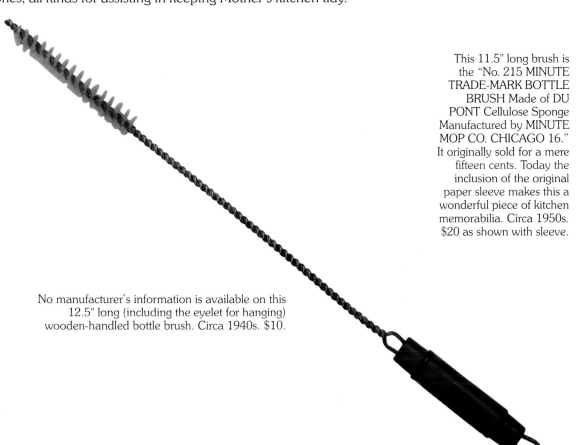

This 11.5" long brush is the "No. 215 MINUTE TRADE-MARK BOTTLE BRUSH Made of DU PONT Cellulose Sponge Manufactured by MINUTE MOP CO. CHICAGO 16." It originally sold for a mere fifteen cents. Today the inclusion of the original paper sleeve makes this a wonderful piece of kitchen memorabilia. Circa 1950s. $20 as shown with sleeve.

No manufacturer's information is available on this 12.5" long (including the eyelet for hanging) wooden-handled bottle brush. Circa 1940s. $10.

Ten cents purchased a "METAL TEXTILE CORP. ROSELLE, N.J. U.S.A. CHORE KNOB." The red wooden knob is 1" tall and the copper scrubbing material is about 3.5" in diameter. The design allowed one to scrub without actually touching the coarse copper wire. Circa 1940s. $20 each.

A 23" long green-handled brush was used to clean radiators. There is no manufacturer's information regarding this brush. Circa 1930s. $18.

This "Whisk-Off" plastic brush has bright red nylon bristles and is marked "MADE IN U.S.A. 4 MODGLISS CO. INC. LOS ANGELES 41 CALIF." Circa late 1950s. $10.

An advertisement is worn from a 5.5" wooden-handled whisk broom that has nylon bristles. Circa 1950s. $10.

There is no manufacturer's information on a 5.25" wide, 6.5" long crumb and lint brush with hand painted embellishments. Circa 1950s. $12.

This is the underside of the crumb and lint brush.

Measuring only 12" in length, a diminutive mop has no manufacturer's information. Circa 1930s. $20.

Cookie Cutters

The first part of this section is devoted to hard plastic cookie cutters. Collectors prefer those made by HRM, LOEW, and LOMA and look for a marking indicating that the item under consideration for purchase was American-made. Trends are beginning to change and some collectors will no long reject cookie cutters that were made in Hong Kong. The one word all collectors seem to agree upon passing by: China. This indicates contemporary merchandise; at least those from Hong Kong are already about thirty years old.

Although most cookie cutters are purchased as part of a collection, some will be used. Spraying a hard plastic cookie cutter with PAM® or another cooking spray will prevent dough from sticking to the nooks and crevices that define the shape.

Three HRM animal cookie cutters are all marked "MADE IN U.S.A." The rooster is 3.25" head to toe, the turkey is 3" from the top of the tail to the toe, and the duck is 3.25" head to toe. Circa 1950s-early 1960s. $5 each.

HRM manufactured these Christmas cookie cutters that are all marked "MADE IN U.S.A." The sizes are as follows: ornament, 3.25"; Santa's head, just over 3.25"; tree, 4"; Santa, 3.5"; wreath, 3.25"; bells, 2.75"; angel, 3.25"; snowman, 3.75"; reindeer, 3.5"; package, 3". Circa 1950s-early 1960s. $3-5 each.

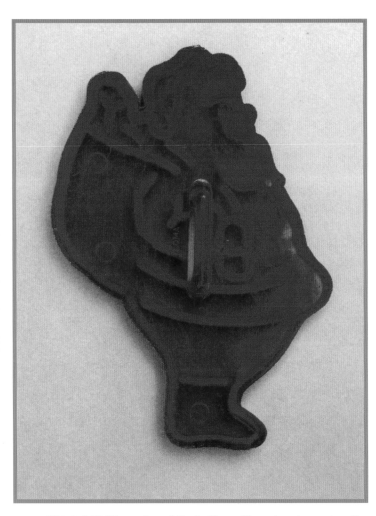

Three of the four rabbit cookie cutters are HRM products. The rabbit head is 4" x 2" and is marked "HRM MADE IN U.S.A." The rabbit up on hind legs is 4.5" x 1.75" and is unmarked but assumed to be American-made. The curled, resting rabbit is 3.75" x 2.25" and is marked "HRM MADE IN U.S.A." The rabbit reaching up measures 3.75" from nose to tail and is marked "HRM MADE IN U.S.A." Circa 1950s-early 1960s. $5 each.

This is LOMA's version of Santa Claus. There is only one handle and he is facing the opposite direction of HRM's Santa. LOMA's Santa is about 1/2" larger than HRM's Santa measuring almost 4" head to toe. Circa 1950s-early 1960s. $5.

Both the 3.75" cat and 3.5" dog are HRM cookie cutters. As the dog is a Scottie, it is particularly popular and a cross-collectible among cookie cutter collectors, kitchen collectors, and Scottish Terrier collectors. Circa 1950s-early 1960s. Cat, $5; Scottie, $8.

There are no manufacturers' marks on the 4" camel, 3.75" horse, and 3.75" donkey. Circa 1950s-early 1960s. $5 each.

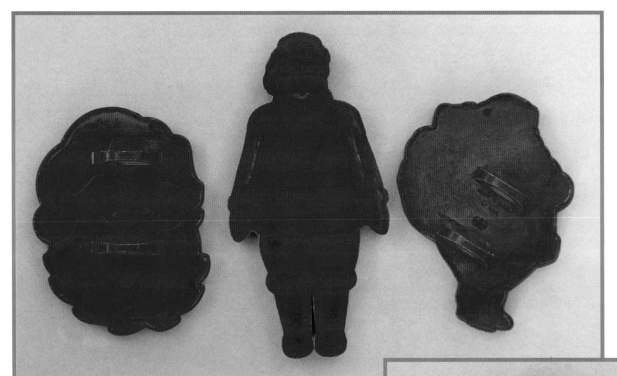

Three different Santas have three different markings. The Santa head is marked "HRM MADE IN U.S.A." and is 3.5" x 2.75". The middle standing Santa is 4.75" x 2.25" and is marked "PAT. PEND." Santa with a pack is marked "MADE IS U.S.A. PAT. PEND. HRM EDUCATIONAL PRODUCTS NY 18" and is 3.5" x 2.75". Circa 1950s-early 1960s. $5 each.

Marked "Betty Crocker GINGERBREAD MIX MADE IN U.S.A.," the red cookie cutter is quite unusual while the blue one is relatively common in comparison. Circa 1950s-early 1960s. Blue, $5; red, $10.

All three HRM cookie cutters include "MADE IN U.S.A." The Jack-o-lantern is 3" x 2.75", the birthday cake is 3" x 3", and the musical staff is 2.5" x 3.75". Circa 1950s-early 1960s. Jack-o-lantern, $8; birthday cake, $3; staff, $15.

These HRM cookie cutters are all about 3.5" tall. Hey, Diddle Diddle, the Cat and the Fiddle is marked "HRM MADE IN U.S.A.," the cowboy is marked "HRM U.S.A.," and Mary, Mary Quite Contrary is marked "HRM MADE IN U.S.A." Circa 1950s-early 1960s. $15 each.

59

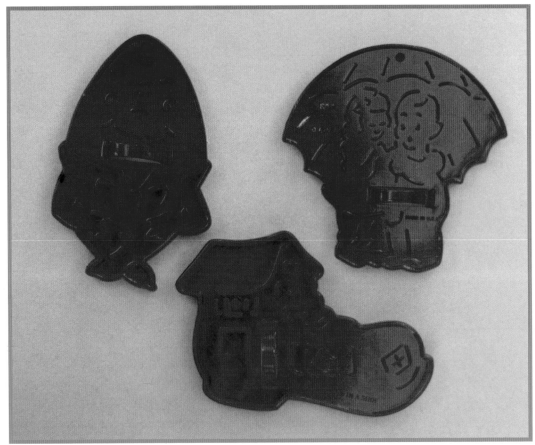

Shown are more nursery rhyme cookie cutters: Humpty Dumpty, The Old Woman in a Shoe, and Rain, Rain Go Away. All are marked "MADE IN U.S.A. HRM." Circa 1950s-early 1960s. $15 each.

The 4" x 2.25" clown is part of a circus set. This is marked "PAT. PEND." Circa 1950s-early 1960s. $15.

60

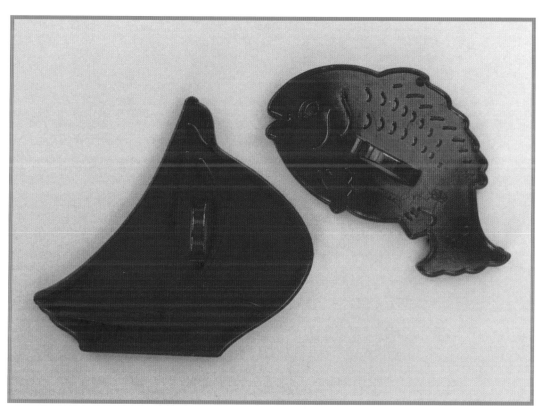

The fish and sailboat are both about 4" and marked "HRM MADE IN U.S.A." Circa 1950s-early 1960s. $15 each.

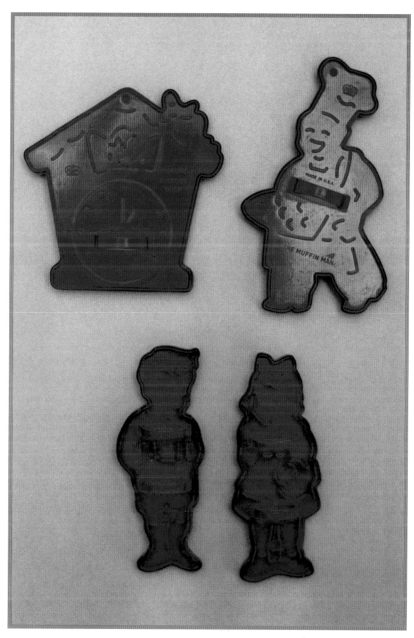

More nursery rhymes are represented with Hickory Dickory Dock, The Muffin Man, and Hansel and Gretel. All are marked with the HRM symbol and "MADE IN U.S.A." The children are additionally marked "PAT. PEND." Circa 1950s-early 1960s. Clock and baker, $15 each; children, $12 each.

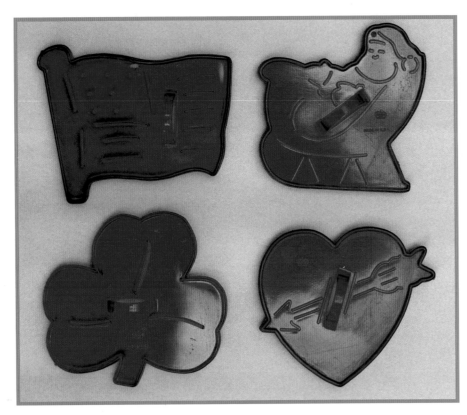

Holidays are an excellent opportunity for cookie baking. These HRM cookie cutters will assist in creating a festive mood. Circa 1950s-early 1960s. $10 each.

The church and locomotive are both marked "HRM MADE IN U.S.A." and are about 3.5" wide. Circa 1950s-early 1960s. $8 each.

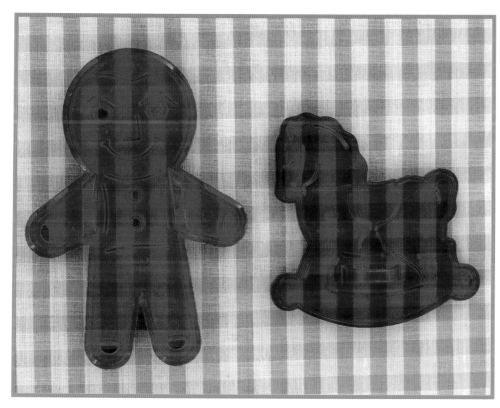

The 4.5" tall Gingerbread Man is marked "DESIGN PAT. 127026" and the 3" wide rocking horse is marked "HRM MADE IN U.S.A." Circa 1950s-early 1960s. $8 each.

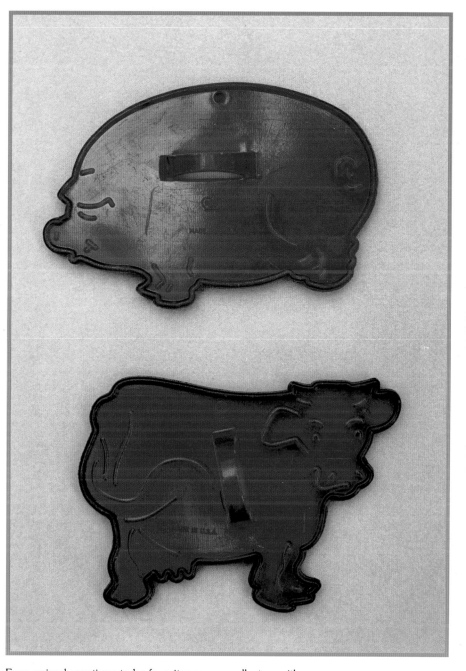

Farm animals continue to be favorites among collectors with a "country" theme. These 3.5" wide HRM cookie cutters will add to a pastoral theme to any kitchen. Circa 1950s-early 1960s. $15 each.

Hutzler Manufacturing Company of Long Island City, NY created several sets of plastic cookie cutters. Shown is the "401 Bridge Set" featuring the four suits of cards. The handle of each is marked "HUTZLER 3 PATENT PENDING." Circa 1950s. $2 each. Add $15 for the box.

The back of the box illustrates the six sets and combinations of sets that Hutzler offered. Circa 1950s. $2 each.

Hutzler's Plastic Cookie Cutters may be purchased in sets and combination of sets listed below

401 — Bridge Set   **405 — Animal Set**

409 — Standard Set

819 — Bridge and Standard Set

859 — Animal and Standard Set

114 — 14 Piece Cookie Set

Robin Hood Flour offered a variety of plastic cookie cutters as premiums to promote baking and in particular the use of their product. Today Robin Hood Flour cookie cutters are among the most valuable of the plastic cookie cutters. The 4" x 1.5" blue cutter is marked "Robin Hood Flour MAID MARIAN MADE IN U.S.A." The 4" x 2.25" red cookie cutter is marked "Robin Hood Flour CASTLE TOWER MADE IN U.S.A." The green cookie cutter is marked "Robin Hood Flour FRIAR TUCK MADE IN U.S.A." Circa 1950s. $20 each.

Serious collectors will want every version of cookie cutter available. Shown are two cookie cutters that are the same except for color. They are identically marked with "Robin Hood Flour CRUSADER MADE IN U.S.A." Circa 1950s-early 1960s. $20 each.

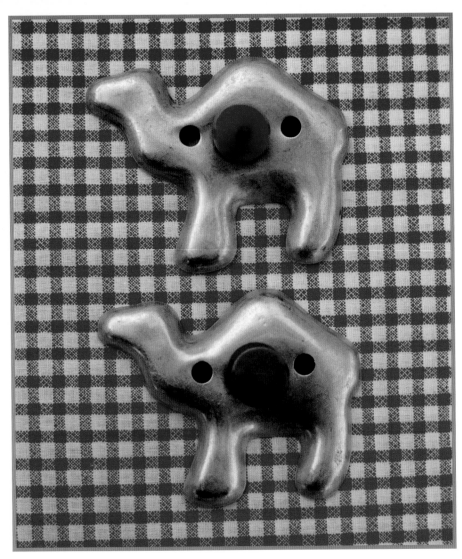

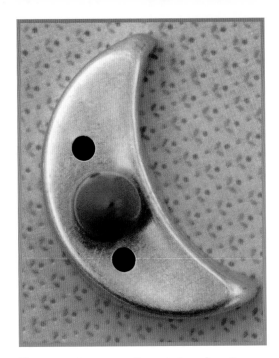

The crescent moon continues to be a favorite with collectors and this 3" example has a green "bullet" or "acorn" handle. Circa 1930s. $15.

Camels are shown with the "bullet" or "acorn" handles that are found in red or green wood. These are 3.25" across and 2.5" tall at the hump. Circa 1930s. $15 each.

In the 1990s wooden-handled cookie cutters were the most popular. Today cookie cutters with metal handles are more in favor and therefore more valuable than some wooden-handled cutters such as the heart, circle, spade, diamond, and club. This 4.25" long lion is one of several animals to be collected. Circa 1930s. $8.

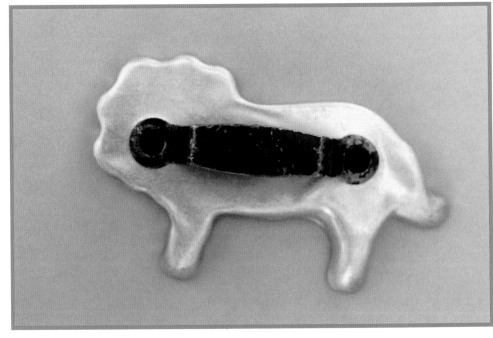

Coring Tools

Many collectors overlook the seldom-used coring tool when seeking to add to a collection. In the days of canning fruit or baking pies from scratch these were invaluable as one needed to remove the core from apples, pears, and so on. Today these tasks are passé and the tools that assisted in their completion are often not recognized, needed, or wanted.

Among the vast array of kitchen tools to be collected it seems as though more original packaging is available for coring tools than for any other gadget. Perhaps even our grandmothers found them less serviceable than a simple paring knife and pushed them to the back of a drawer, forgotten.

Fifty cents bought a 4.5" long Vitex fruit and vegetable corer in plastic with a red wooden handle. Circa late 1940s. $5 without box, $15 with box.

Renwal, the maker of plastic doll house furniture, produced this tool that assisted in the preparation of a number of fresh fruits and vegetables as listed on a side panel of the box.

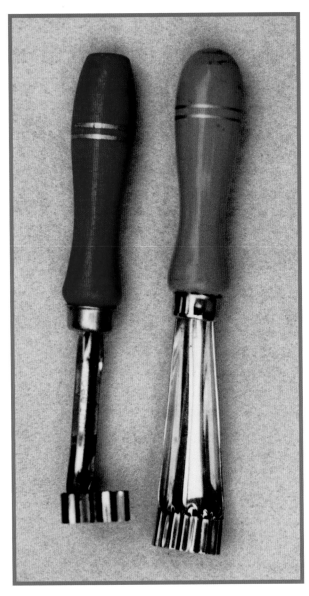

Two silver stripes indicate that the British company, Nutbrown, manufactured these tools. The 6" long red coring tool is marked "A NUTBROWN PRODUCT MADE IN ENGLAND" and the 6.5" long blue coring tool is marked "Nutbrown BUTTER PAT MAKER AND APPLE CORER MADE IN ENGLAND." Circa 1940s. $15 each.

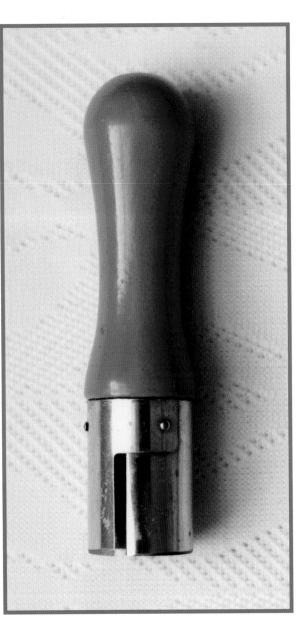

A wider diameter helps to distinguish a 5.25" long "DURABILT GRAPE FRUIT CORER" from other coring tools. Circa 1930s. $10.

Blue handles as well as a unique design help to distinguish the 6.25" long Utility Corer marked "MADE IN USA PAT. NO. 1638798." Circa 1927. $15.

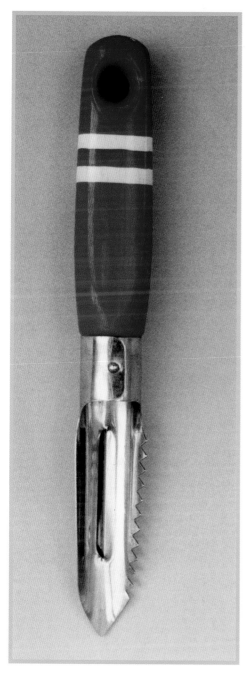

A & J manufactured this 6.5" coring and peeling tool that is marked "STAINLESS STEEL A & J MADE IN UNITED STATES OF AMERICA." Circa 1930s-1940s. $12.

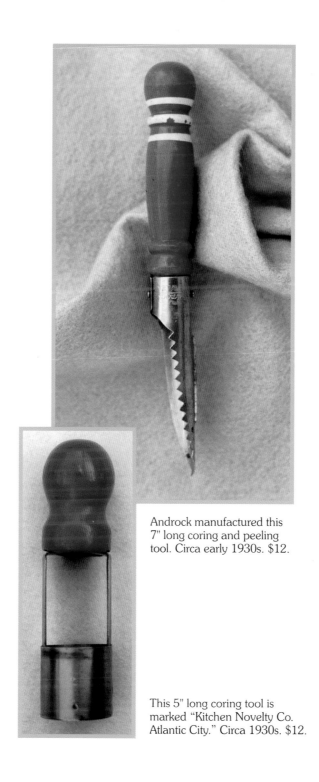

Androck manufactured this 7" long coring and peeling tool. Circa early 1930s. $12.

This 5" long coring tool is marked "Kitchen Novelty Co. Atlantic City." Circa 1930s. $12.

A 6" long tool by Boye, patented in 1916, has the directions engraved in metal: "push 3/4 thru apple twist and remove forming cup to hold sugar." Circa late 1920s. $12.

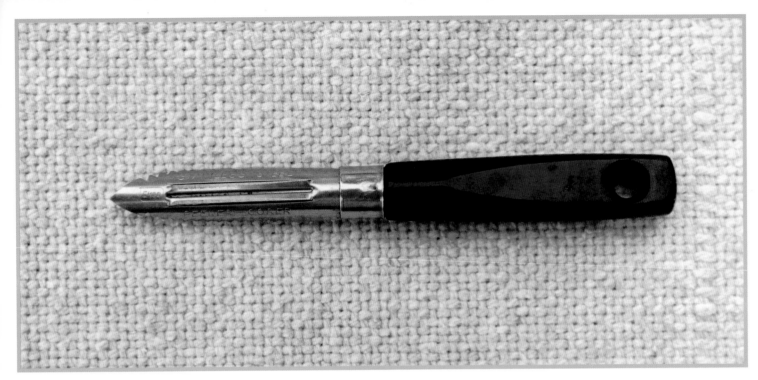

Although not easily found in pristine condition, black-handled kitchen tools are relatively unpopular and thus of lower value than counterparts in other colors. This 7" long coring and peeling tool is marked "EKCO U.S.A. STAIN-LESS STEEL PEELER-CORER." Circa 1930s. $8.

Marked "WB" over another "W," this 6.5" American-made tool features an especially attractive handle treatment. Circa 1930s. $12, as shown with a cracked handle.

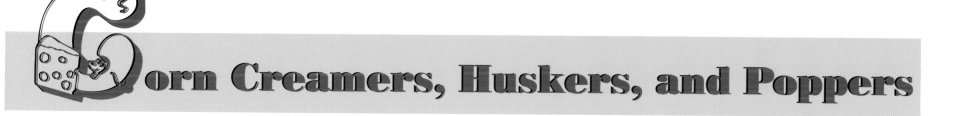

Corn creamers and huskers are such obscure kitchen tools they are usually misidentified. Few collectors purchase these tools for actual use, while other gadgets are often purchased for aesthetics as well as for use. Conversely, corn poppers are easy to identify and fun to use.

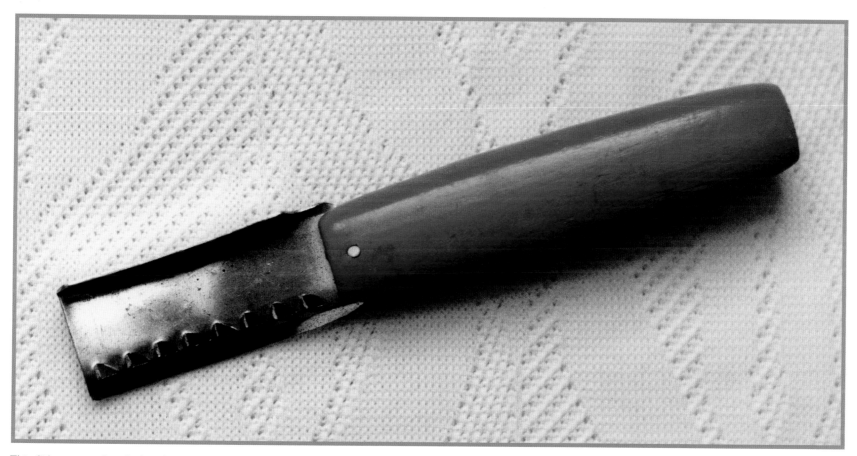

This 6" long green-handled tool is marked "CORN CREAMER PAT. NO 1345456 WALTER OLCOTT CO. MANCHESTER CONN." The patent date is 1920, but the green handle makes this no older than 1927. Circa late 1920s. $15.

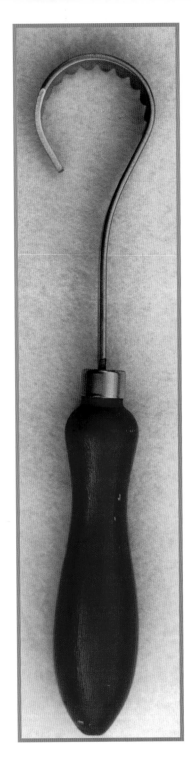

This 26.5" long corn popper is constructed with mesh and has no manufacturer's information. Circa 1930s. $18.

There are no markings on this 8.25" long red-handled corn husker. Circa late 1920s. $20.

The "Ripple Bottom Popper" is 26.25" long. The original label explains that "every kernel pops… the (metal) ripple bottom turns the corn." Circa 1930s. $25 as shown with the original label.

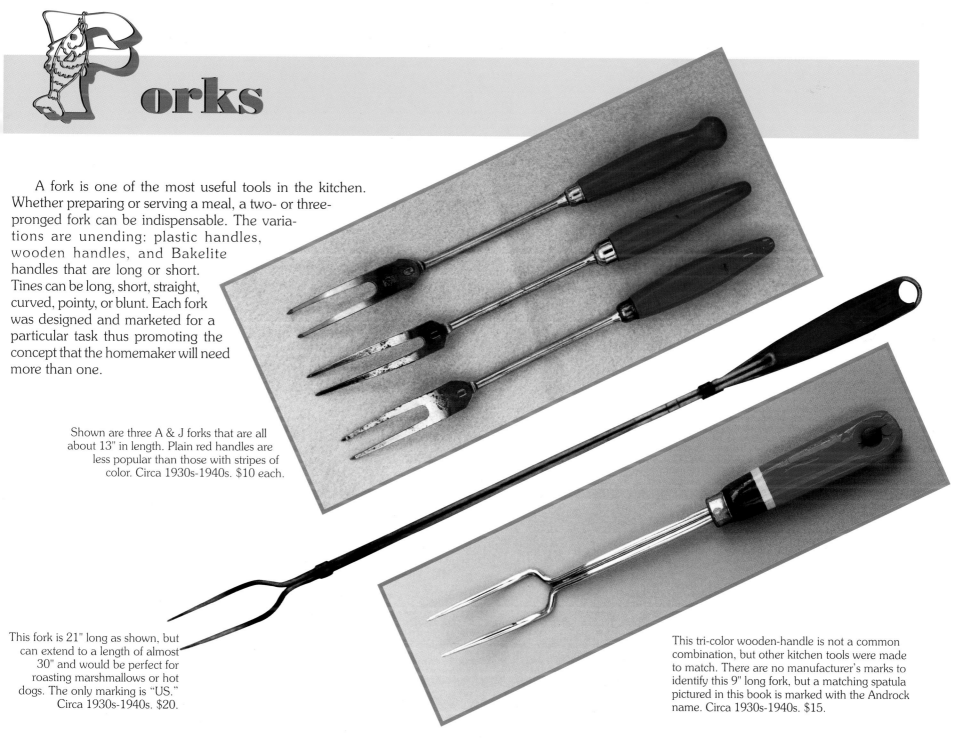

P orks

A fork is one of the most useful tools in the kitchen. Whether preparing or serving a meal, a two- or three-pronged fork can be indispensable. The variations are unending: plastic handles, wooden handles, and Bakelite handles that are long or short. Tines can be long, short, straight, curved, pointy, or blunt. Each fork was designed and marketed for a particular task thus promoting the concept that the homemaker will need more than one.

Shown are three A & J forks that are all about 13" in length. Plain red handles are less popular than those with stripes of color. Circa 1930s-1940s. $10 each.

This fork is 21" long as shown, but can extend to a length of almost 30" and would be perfect for roasting marshmallows or hot dogs. The only marking is "US." Circa 1930s-1940s. $20.

This tri-color wooden-handle is not a common combination, but other kitchen tools were made to match. There are no manufacturer's marks to identify this 9" long fork, but a matching spatula pictured in this book is marked with the Androck name. Circa 1930s-1940s. $15.

Another A & J fork that is almost 13" long has a slightly different handle design. Circa 1930s-1940s. $10.

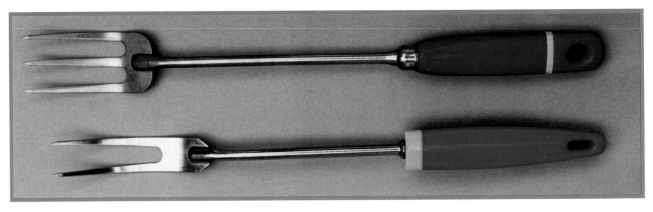

The three-pronged fork is 13.25" long and marked "A & J MADE IN UNITED STATES OF AMERICA." The two-pronged fork is 12.5" long with a triangular plastic handle and is marked "EKCO ETERNA STAINLESS STEEL MADE IN U.S.A." On the shaft additional markings state "STAINLESS STEEL THROUGHOUT." Wooden handle, Circa 1930s-1940s; plastic handle late 1940s-1950s. $12 each.

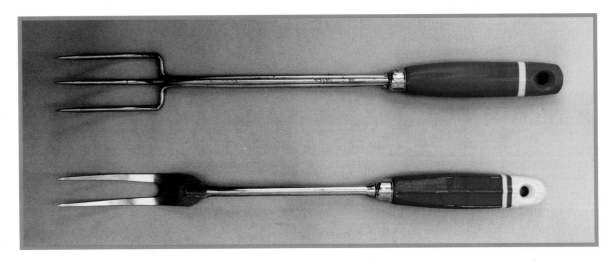

Both forks are about 13" long and marked "MADE IN U.S.A." The two-pronged fork is also marked A & J. Circa 1930s-1940s. $12 each.

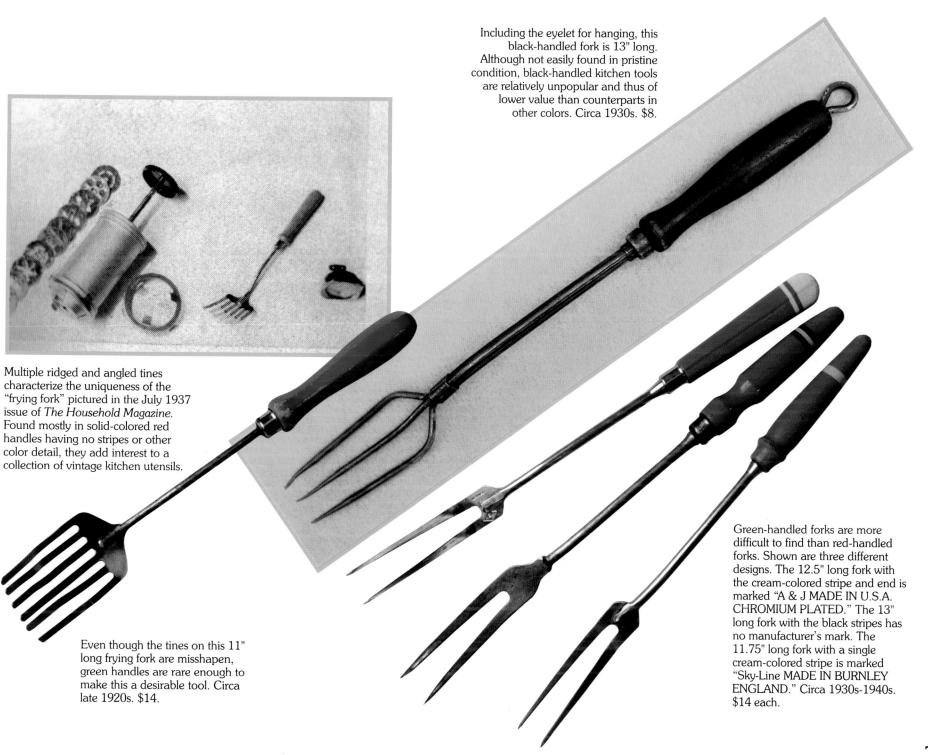

Including the eyelet for hanging, this black-handled fork is 13" long. Although not easily found in pristine condition, black-handled kitchen tools are relatively unpopular and thus of lower value than counterparts in other colors. Circa 1930s. $8.

Multiple ridged and angled tines characterize the uniqueness of the "frying fork" pictured in the July 1937 issue of *The Household Magazine*. Found mostly in solid-colored red handles having no stripes or other color detail, they add interest to a collection of vintage kitchen utensils.

Even though the tines on this 11" long frying fork are misshapen, green handles are rare enough to make this a desirable tool. Circa late 1920s. $14.

Green-handled forks are more difficult to find than red-handled forks. Shown are three different designs. The 12.5" long fork with the cream-colored stripe and end is marked "A & J MADE IN U.S.A. CHROMIUM PLATED." The 13" long fork with the black stripes has no manufacturer's mark. The 11.75" long fork with a single cream-colored stripe is marked "Sky-Line MADE IN BURNLEY ENGLAND." Circa 1930s-1940s. $14 each.

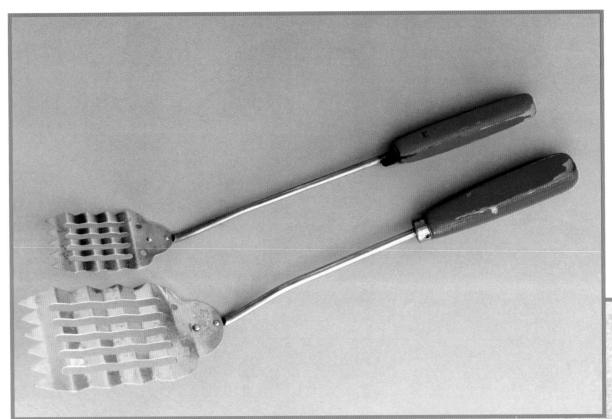

Variations on a theme, here are a 12.25" long and a 13.5" long "Becky Porter's Frying Fork." Each is marked "STAINLESS PAT. 1723507," a patent from 1929. Circa 1929. $14 each.

Androck manufactured Bakelite "Bullet-handled" kitchen utensils such as this 12.25" long fork. Marked "STAINLESS STEEL MADE IN U.S.A.," the bullet handle is one of the most popular design styles with collectors of Bakelite kitchenware. Circa 1930s. $25.

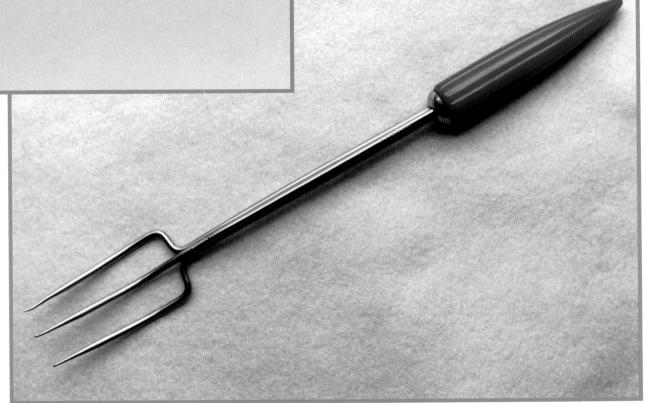

rench Fry Cutters

Advertisements praise the ease in which a single potato is transformed into a serving of French Fries. Today's consumers are rediscovering this handy tool that will provide multiple, uniform pieces of virtually anything that will fit. Care must be taken to select French Fry Cutters that are free from rust and deterioration. An abundant enough quantity has survived allowing the ability to be discriminating when shopping, and so many are still found with original packaging that one might deduce they were not particularly popular when introduced.

The mechanism pictured in this advertisement from the November 1950 issue of *The American Home* shows the most common French Fry Cutter. The wooden handle can be found predominantly in red, but black, white, and green are not impossible to find. Wooden handles in blue were made, but these are difficult to find. Circa late 1930s- early 1950s. $12. Add more for original packaging depending on condition.

Almost a year later and the price remains the same as shown in the July 1951 issue of *The American Home.*

European manufacturers provided a one-piece device for creating French Fries, sixty-four to be exact. Marked "TOMADO HOLLAND" this design requires a measure of brute strength making it harder to use as well as harder to find. Circa late 1940s-early 1950s. $15.

arnishing Tools

What separates humans from beasts? It is more than an opposable thumb; we garnish our food prior to its consumption. Artistic presentation can take a plain serving of food and raise it to high epicurean standards.

An interesting array of tools was created to allow the homemaker to transform an otherwise uninteresting portion of food into a work of art, or at least a more interesting if not delightful meal.

It is worth noting that cookie cutters were also marketed as sandwich cutters and therefore could almost be included herein. Additionally, some garnishing tools are pictured with coring tools.

A 6.5" "NUTBROWN FRUIT DECORATOR" from England assists in the process of cutting decorative edges on melons, grapefruit, apples, and more. Two silver stripes always indicate a Nutbrown kitchen tool. Circa 1940s. $15 each.

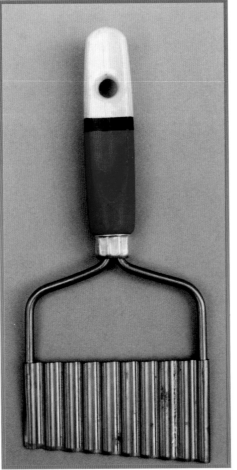

Tri-colored wooden handles are difficult to find in any condition, and this 7" "Sky-Line" garnishing tool is in pristine condition. Made in England, there are additional kitchen tools with this red, black, and white handle. Circa 1930s-1940s. $15.

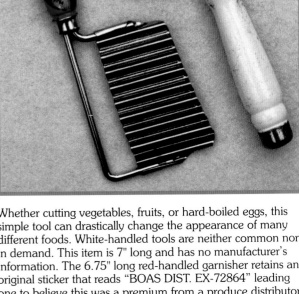

Whether cutting vegetables, fruits, or hard-boiled eggs, this simple tool can drastically change the appearance of many different foods. White-handled tools are neither common nor in demand. This item is 7" long and has no manufacturer's information. The 6.75" long red-handled garnisher retains an original sticker that reads "BOAS DIST. EX-72864" leading one to believe this was a premium from a produce distributor. Circa 1950s. White, $5; red, $12.

Graters

Truly one of the earliest kitchen tools, graters from the 1800s can be worth hundreds of dollars depending upon their designs, but collectors often overlook graters from the late 1920s through the 1950s. Occasionally a grater is purchased to be used as a backboard on which smaller kitchen collectibles will be glued or wired to create a decoration.

The advent of blenders and then food processors has further contributed to the demise of the lowly grater.

What follows is a presentation of stationary and mechanical graters. Perhaps some interest will be sparked after viewing the array of designs and collectors will decide that graters are great!

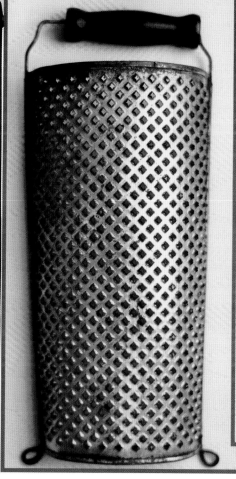

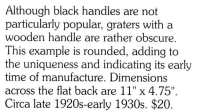

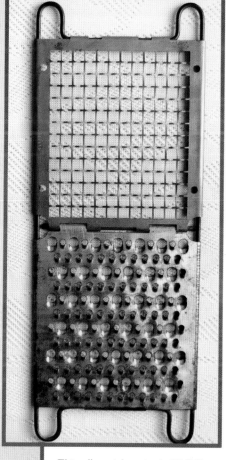

A flat 11" x 4" grater is marked "SIMPLEX MADE BY DANDEE INC. STURGIS, MICH. IN U.S.A." The red handle adds to its appeal, but deterioration makes this unsuitable for use. Circa 1930s. $15.

Although black handles are not particularly popular, graters with a wooden handle are rather obscure. This example is rounded, adding to the uniqueness and indicating its early time of manufacture. Dimensions across the flat back are 11" x 4.75". Circa late 1920s-early 1930s. $20.

This all-metal grater is 10.25" x 4.75" with an additional 1" extension in each corner. Designed to sit on a bowl when being used, this is marked "A & J MADE IN U.S.A. U.S. PAT. NO. 2252859." The lack of a colored handle results in this being of limited interest to most collectors. Circa 1941. $8.

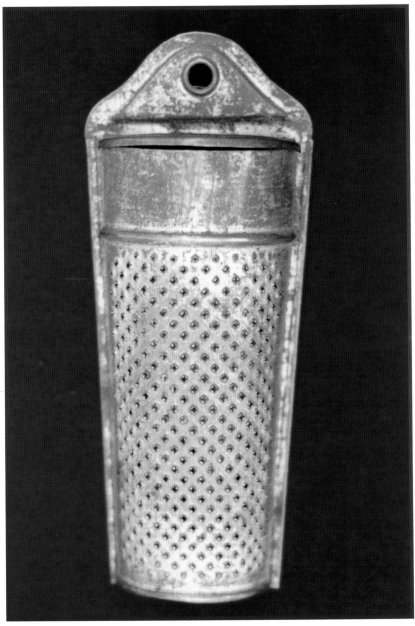

After World War II many American-made kitchen tools were manufactured with plastic, the modern material of the post-war era. Two "Vitex Safety Graters" that originally sold for $1.00 each are shown with their original boxes. The white grater is 5.5" x 7.5" and the dark green grater is 4.5" x 7.25". Both graters are marked "A RENWAL PRODUCT MADE IN U.S.A." Renwal is known for their line of plastic doll house toys. Circa late 1940s. $5 each without box, $15 each with box.

Nutmeg graters with intricate and interesting mechanisms were produced prior to the Depression Era. The simple 6" tall metal nutmeg grater from England that is pictured here is as unsophisticated as they come and still relatively easy to find. Circa 1940s. $15.

rinders

Meat grinders are usually of little or no interest to collectors of kitchenware from the 1920s through 1950s. Even when found (rarely) with a colored wooden handle grinders are normally overlooked.

Other grinders are more fascinating and interesting to collectors. An assortment of materials, colors, and designs were utilized and today we are left with much from which to select.

Check the Chopper Jar section for more examples.

This 3.25" tall D.R.G.M. German grinder in red and white hard plastic is quite unusual. The red lid screws on and off to add or retrieve the item being reduced. Circa 1950s. $30.

There are no other markings on the 4" x 1.75" x 2.75" metal grinder other than that which is shown in this image. The green lid slides to allow the placement of the items to be reduced. For collectors of green and cream kitchenware this would be a prized possession. Circa late 1920s. $60.

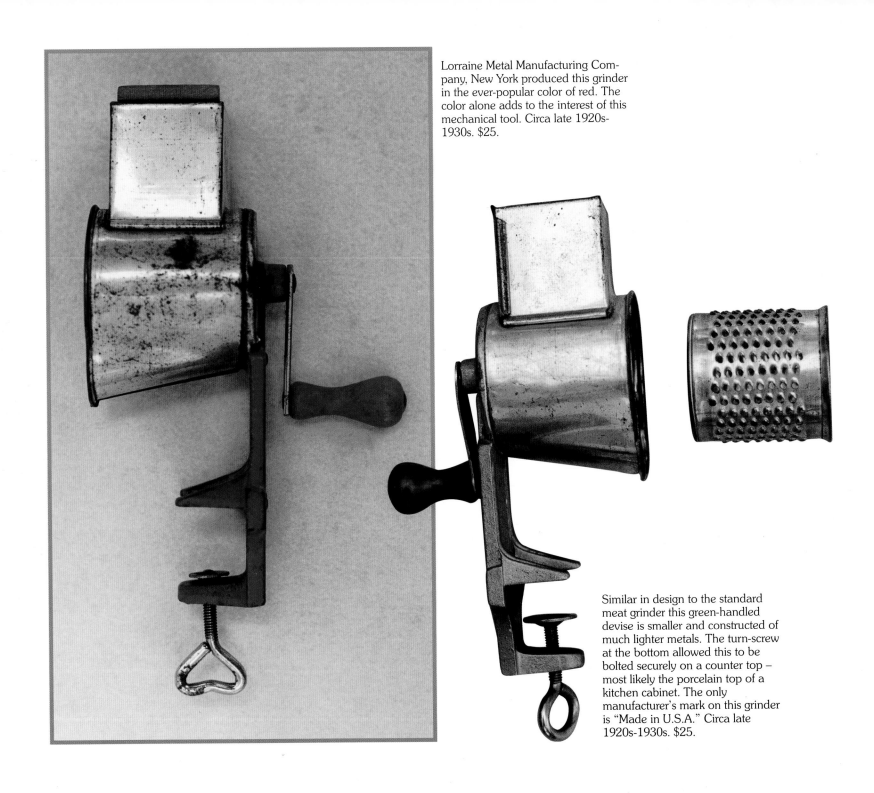

Lorraine Metal Manufacturing Company, New York produced this grinder in the ever-popular color of red. The color alone adds to the interest of this mechanical tool. Circa late 1920s-1930s. $25.

Similar in design to the standard meat grinder this green-handled devise is smaller and constructed of much lighter metals. The turn-screw at the bottom allowed this to be bolted securely on a counter top – most likely the porcelain top of a kitchen cabinet. The only manufacturer's mark on this grinder is "Made in U.S.A." Circa late 1920s-1930s. $25.

When collectors think of nutmeat grinders they often picture a glass jar with a metal grinding apparatus that screws on top. Often the manufacturers of the metal assembly produced additional kitchenware such as sifters to match. The same lithographed design was sometimes produced in an array of colors to match a homemaker's kitchen décor. There is a patent number too worn to read on this 5" tall nutmeat grinder. Circa 1930s-1940s. $12.

This 5.25" tall Androck "UNIFORM NUTMEAT GRINDER" has a patent date from 1935. The tulip decal is not original, but the red stripes on the glass reservoir enhance the value. Circa 1930s-1940s. $18.

Ice Picks, Choppers, Crushers, and Breakers

Before refrigerators there were iceboxes and to utilize a big block of ice smaller pieces would be chipped free using an ice pick. Most commonly found with wooden handles, some had metal handles; they needed to withstand the pounding required to split off a piece of ice.

Much of the value of an ice pick is based upon the advertisement that might be on the handle.

Ice choppers, crushers, and breakers assisted in reducing large pieces of ice into sizes suitable for use in a tumbler or pitcher. An interesting assortment of tools was created to accomplish this.

Ice choppers can be distinguished from ice picks because of the multiple prongs that ease the process of creating smaller pieces of ice. They may also have a spring-loaded action that compresses the shaft when striking ice. This red-handled ice chopper is 9" long but compresses to 7.75" when pressure is applied. There are no manufacturer's marks on this five-prong tool. Circa late 1920s-1930s. $8.

The unusual handle does not enhance the value of a 7.25" long ice pick. Circa late 1920s-1930s. $8.

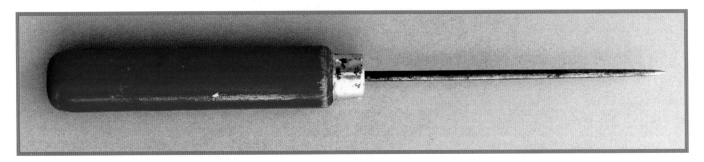

A plain red-handled ice pick has little value. This is 8.5" long and due to the deterioration of the metal the manufacturer's markings are impossible to read. Circa late 1920s-1930s. $8.

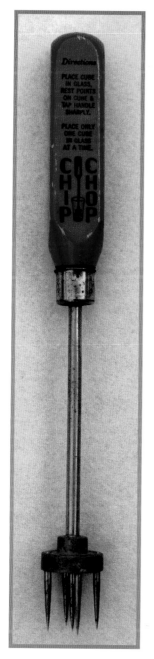

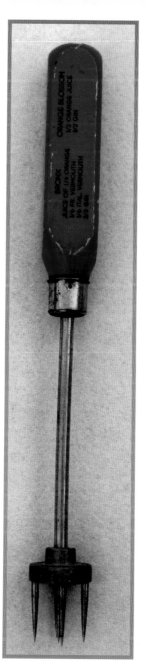

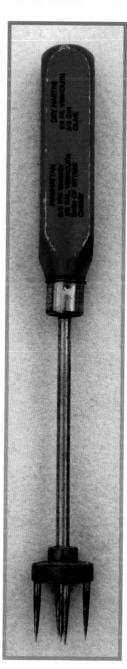

The 8.75" long "CHIP CHOP" has recipes for cocktails on three sides of the wooden handle. Circa late 1920s-1930s. $8.

Here is the recipe for Bronx.

Manhattan anyone?

A recipe for an Old Fashioned is on this old-fashioned kitchen tool.

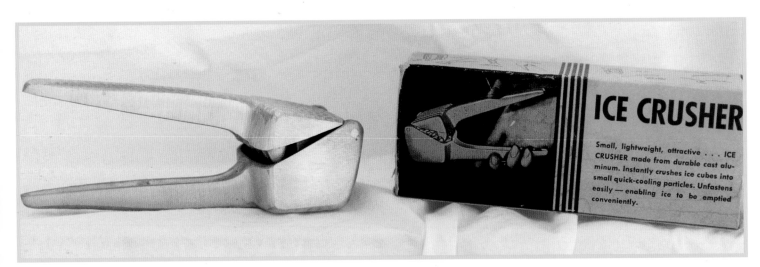

ICE CRUSHER

Small, lightweight, attractive . . . ICE CRUSHER made from durable cast aluminum. Instantly crushes ice cubes into small quick-cooling particles. Unfastens easily — enabling ice to be emptied conveniently.

Small pieces of ice can be created more quickly with this aluminum ice crusher. The only manufacturing information is an "E" inside the receptacle and "PAT. PEND" inside a handle. Circa 1930s. $10, add $10 for the box.

Other products ranging from a mailbox to an orange juicer are advertised on a side panel of the package.

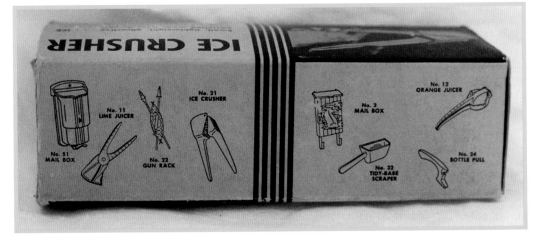

Designed to make the ice pick obsolete, the "LIGHTNING ICE CUBE BREAKER" featured a mechanism similar to a meat grinder. Small particles of ice would fall into a glass reservoir that was actually a refrigerator dish. One could create chipped ice and store it in the same container into which it fell for only $3.75 as offered in the December 9, 1933 *The Saturday Evening Post.*

In the June 1938 issue of *The American Home* an even more modern approach to ice was featured as the number one item in "NEW and IMPORTANT for YOUR KITCHEN." The "Du-More ice cuber…makes perfect ice cubes in three minutes – useful every day and grand when thirsty guests arrive."

Knife Holders

Past kitchens had virtually no counter space so walls were utilized as fully as possible. While contemporary kitchens may include a knife block that is placed on a counter, in the 1920s and 1930s a knife block was hung on the wall.

Red and white is the most common color combination for the NUWAY knife holder. Circa 1939-early 1940s. $30.

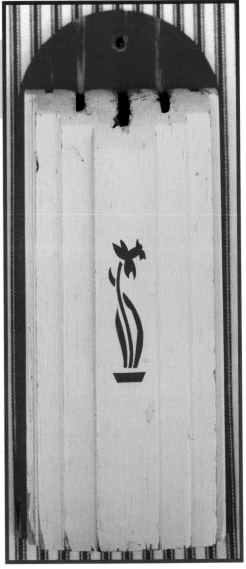

The 9.5" x 4" x 1.75" "NUWAY" knife holder is the most common one seen. It was made in black, red, blue, and green with white and designed to hold five knives. Circa 1939-early 1940s. $30.

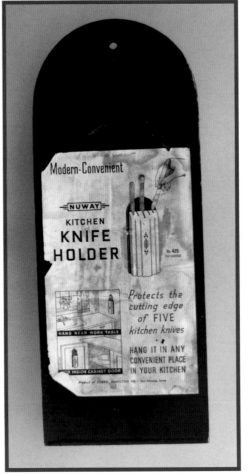

Modern·Convenient

NUWAY
KITCHEN
KNIFE
HOLDER

No. 425 PATENTED

HANG NEAR WORK TABLE

OR INSIDE CABINET DOOR

Protects the cutting edge of FIVE kitchen knives

HANG IT IN ANY CONVENIENT PLACE IN YOUR KITCHEN

It is particularly rewarding to find a knife holder with the original paper label on the back.

By 1940 the NUWAY knife holder could be acquired through the Pillsbury Thrift Star Premiums Program. Shown is the cover of 1940 catalogue.

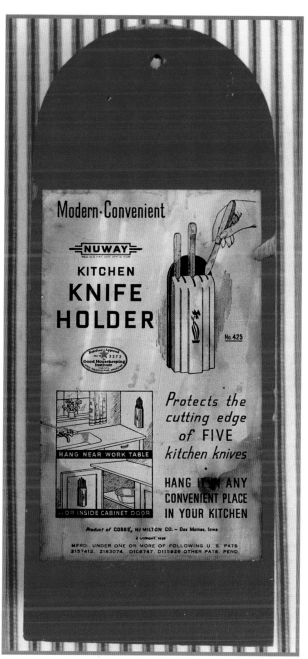

This label is a bit newer than the previous one as now the knife holder had earned the Good Housekeeping Seal of Approval.

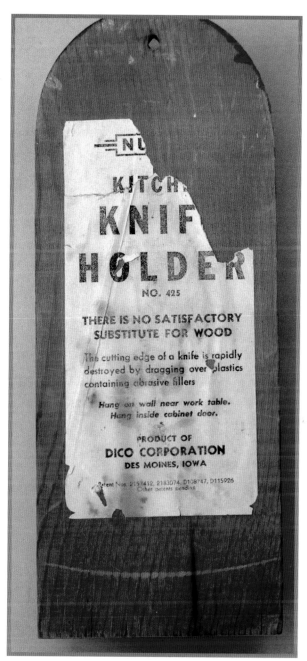

This is probably one of the very earliest labels for the NUWAY knife holder.

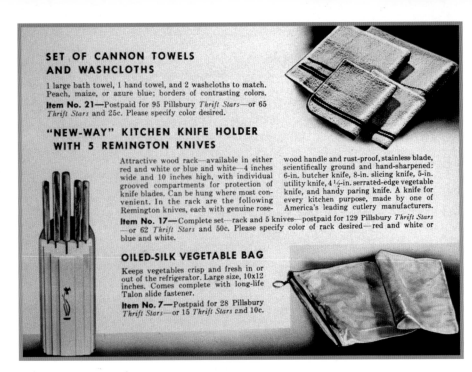

SET OF CANNON TOWELS AND WASHCLOTHS

1 large bath towel, 1 hand towel, and 2 washcloths to match. Peach, maize, or azure blue; borders of contrasting colors.

Item No. 21—Postpaid for 95 Pillsbury *Thrift Stars*—or 65 *Thrift Stars* and 25c. Please specify color desired.

"NEW-WAY" KITCHEN KNIFE HOLDER WITH 5 REMINGTON KNIVES

Attractive wood rack—available in either red and white or blue and white—4 inches wide and 10 inches high, with individual grooved compartments for protection of knife blades. Can be hung where most convenient. In the rack are the following Remington knives, each with genuine rose-wood handle and rust-proof, stainless blade, scientifically ground and hand-sharpened: 6-in. butcher knife, 8-in. slicing knife, 5-in. utility knife, 4½-in. serrated-edge vegetable knife, and handy paring knife. A knife for every kitchen purpose, made by one of America's leading cutlery manufacturers.

Item No. 17—Complete set—rack and 5 knives—postpaid for 129 Pillsbury *Thrift Stars* —or 62 *Thrift Stars* and 50c. Please specify color of rack desired—red and white or blue and white.

OILED-SILK VEGETABLE BAG

Keeps vegetables crisp and fresh in or out of the refrigerator. Large size, 10x12 inches. Comes complete with long-life Talon slide fastener.

Item No. 7—Postpaid for 28 Pillsbury *Thrift Stars*—or 15 *Thrift Stars* and 10c.

Spelled "NEW-WAY," 129 Thrift Stars or 62 Thrift Stars and fifty cents rewarded the homemaker with a knife holder and with a five-piece assortment of Remington knives with rosewood handles and stainless steel blades.

This 10" x 3.5" x 1.75" knife holder also held five knives, but in a rarely-seen configuration. Only remnants of the original paper label have survived, but some important information can be gleaned. This was patented sometime in the 1930s by a Vermont company. NUWAY was a product of DICO Corporation in Iowa, and it is quite possible that this holder preceded it. Circa 1930s. $40.

nives

Probably the single most abundant kitchen tool is the knife. When it is time to cut food, nothing works better. There are different blades for different tasks as well as different handle styles, lengths, and materials.

Knives are such an important kitchen element that when Bakelite was introduced as a consumer-friendly material in the mid-1920s it was utilized as handle material for table knives.

Although not a particularly popular kitchen collectible, several interesting examples are presented, and perhaps this will cut through any apathy.

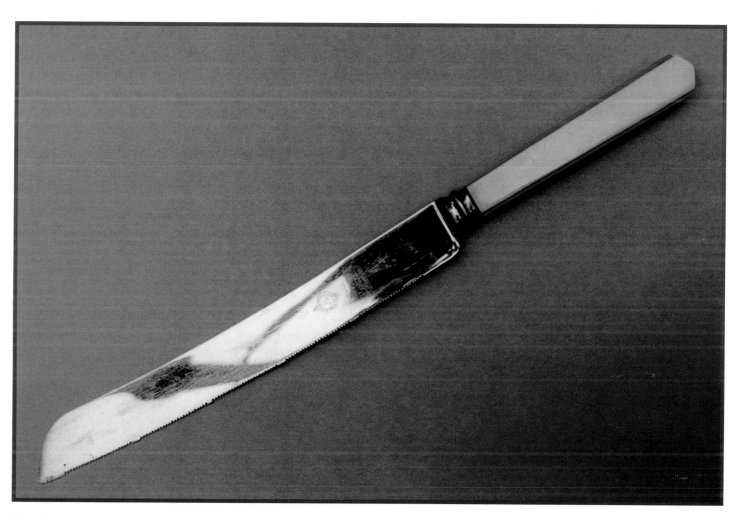

This 12.5" long celluloid-handled knife is marked "Made in Sheffield England Hand Ground Flint Stainless." Truly a high-quality knife, few collectors seek celluloid-handled kitchen items, even when the handle has two colors. Circa late 1920s-1930s. $8.

Although these two-colored handles appear similar to the previous knife, the 8.25" long steak knife and 6.5" long grapefruit knife have Bakelite handles. Both have stainless steel blades. Circa 1930s-1940s. $25 each.

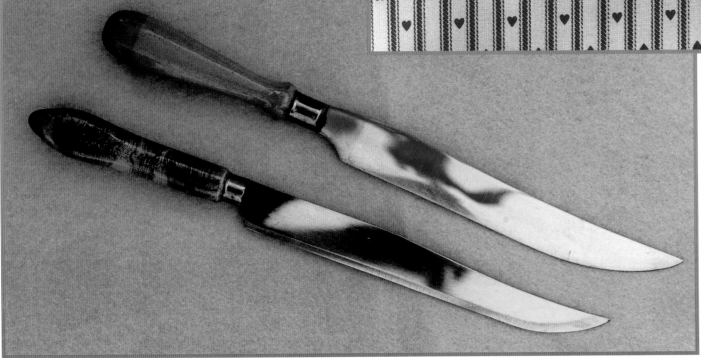

Looking for a wooden handle more colorful than black? Shown are two unique knives that should meet that need. The top knife is gray with a blue/green tip. It is 13" long and marked "A & J STAINLESS." The bottom knife has an end-of-the-day handle: last bits of paint used during the day are used up at the end of the workday creating a colorful and popular handle design. Circa 1930s. Top, $10; bottom, $25.

The wooden handle shown here on a 13.25" long knife is quite rare. One can suppose this color combination was used on other tools, but we have yet to find any. The blade is marked "WB" over another "W." Circa 1930s. $35.

Black handles are not particularly popular, but these knives wonderfully illustrate a variety of blades. The top knife is 13" long and has no manufacturer's information. The other two knives are each 15" in length and feature advertising on their blades. The middle knife is marked "COMPLIMENTS OF E.J. GROSS BAKER SLATEDALE, P.A." and the bottom knife is marked "COMPLIMENTS OF J.D. CARL GENERAL MERCHANDISE OLD ZIONVILLE, PA." Circa late 1920s-early 1930s. $8 each, however those with advertising may be worth more if offered for sale in the geographic regions stated on the blades.

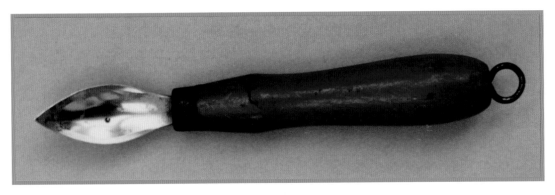

This 5.75" long green-handled knife is designed to remove citrus sections, an obscure job for an obscure knife. Circa late 1920s-1930s. $20.

If you are still struggling with a grapefruit there is always the "Vitex GRAPEFRUIT PREPARER" for only fifty cents. The 6.5" plastic knife is unmarked, but the box assures the user that it is "Ideal for sectioning and Separating meaty Part from Rind." This is "RENWAL PRODUCT NO. 875 A MADE IN U.S.A." Circa late 1940s. $5 without box, $15 with box.

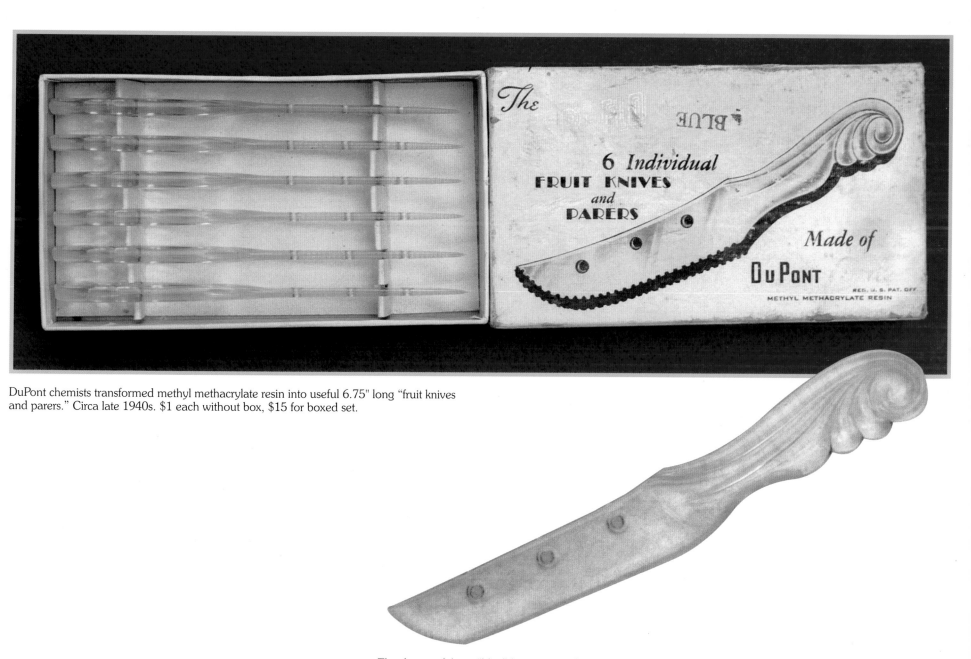

DuPont chemists transformed methyl methacrylate resin into useful 6.75" long "fruit knives and parers." Circa late 1940s. $1 each without box, $15 for boxed set.

The design of these "blue" knives is similar to Depression Glass fruit and cake knives. The holes in the blades were to streamline the cutting process.

One of the earliest STYRON advertisements was in the March 1948 issue of *Better Homes and Gardens*.

Styron, another form of plastic, was an element of many post-World War II kitchen items including the handle of a 10" "Quikut STAINLESS" cleaver. Few collectors show interest in Styron kitchenware at this time. Circa 1950s. $8.

Ladles

Whether called a ladle or a dipper, nothing is better for serving broth, soup, or punch. This rather basic utensil was made in a variety of designs: different materials for the handle, different sizes, different spout configurations, etc.

Do not leave a vintage ladle resting against the side of a hot pot or pan as the handle may burn, scorch, or even melt, depending upon the material from which it was made.

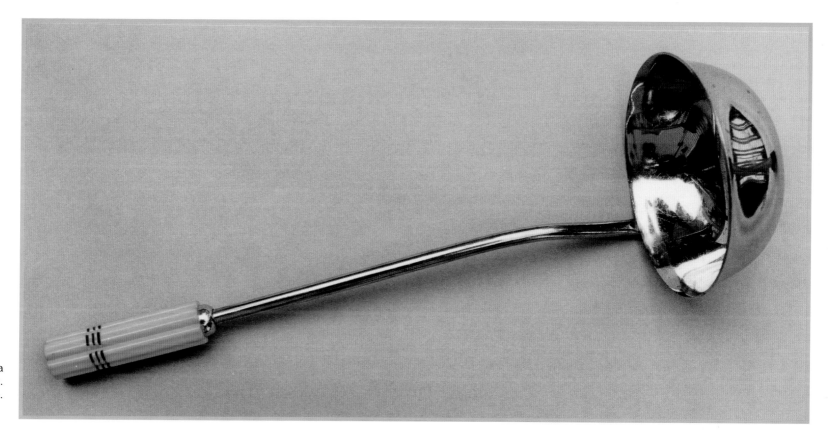

This 11.5" long ladle has a textured Bakelite handle. Circa 1930s-1940s. $35.

Neither of these green wooden-handled ladles have manufacturers' information. They have unique handle and bowl designs. Circa 1930s. $14 each.

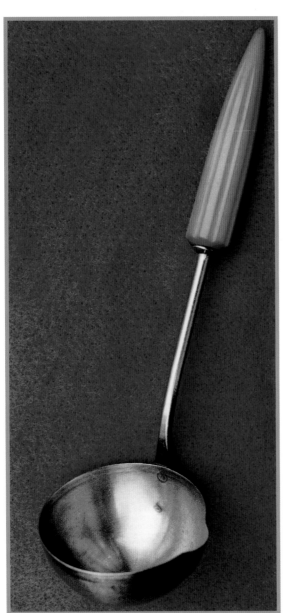

Although there is no manufacturer's information on this 10" long ladle the Bakelite "Bullet" handle was an Androck design. Circa 1930s. $25.

As with the green-handled ladles, an 11" long red-handled ladle has no manufacturer's information. Circa 1930s-1940s. $12.

Marked "Saturn trademark U.R.C. N.Y. U.S.A." this 13" long ladle has holes for straining, a rarely seen design. Circa 1930s. $14.

This 12" long ladle has no manufacturer's information. Circa 1930s. $14.

This 12" long straining ladle is marked "MADE IN UNITED STATES OF AMERICA A & J." Circa 1930s-1940s. $14.

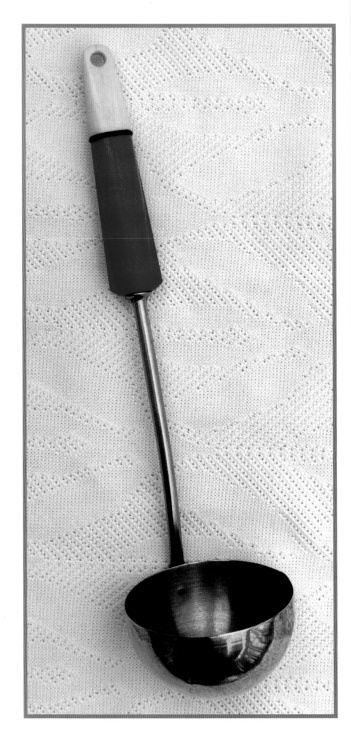

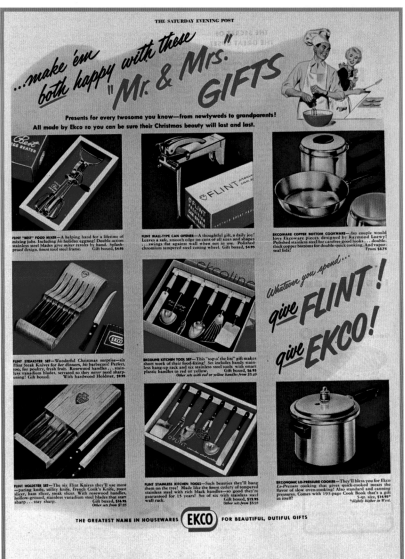

EKCO advertised their white-with-yellow and white-with-red handles in the December 1, 1951 issue of *The Saturday Evening Post.* EKCO also made handles in green and white and blue and white, but less were made and few are found in any condition. The set shown in the advertisement was only $6.95 complete with a gift box.

Plastic was the new modern material of post-war America. The red and white plastic handle of the 11.5" long ladle is the same handle shown in the following advertisement. This is marked "STAINLESS STEEL THROUGHOUT." An advertisement featuring this item is shown in the Spoons section. Circa late 1940s-1950s. $8.

Match Safes

One of the most popular metal kitchen collectible is the match safe. Most were part of complete metalware collections, and some of these sets included more than twenty matching accessories: canisters, bread boxes, sifters, trays, and so on.

The match safe was designed to hang on the wall because counter space in kitchens past was virtually nonexistent; efficient and effective use of wall space was critical.

Condition, design, and color are the most important factors when a collector makes a selection for purchase. If the match safe is part of a set being collected, naturally there would be interest in adding it to the grouping. However, some match safes are simply pleasant to look at and enhance a kitchen décor without the assistance of matching pieces.

Matching canisters, sifters, and more can be found in this fruit design that was made in blue, red, and green. This is a decoration that is not particularly popular with today's collectors. Circa 1930s. $25.

Because the colors aren't vivid, this match safe is not particularly popular. Circa 1930s. $25.

This design was used on a complete line of metal kitchenware. Circa early 1940s. $35.

101

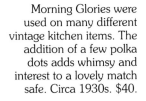

Tulips and other Dutch themes continue to be popular with collectors. This match safe has a variety of matching kitchen items. Circa early 1930s. $40.

White Dogwood blossoms boldly decorate this match safe. Circa 1930s-early 1940s. $40.

Morning Glories were used on many different vintage kitchen items. The addition of a few polka dots adds whimsy and interest to a lovely match safe. Circa 1930s. $40.

Melon Ball Makers

With all of our advances in gadgetry and appliances there is still nothing other than the melon ball maker that can provide these little spheres of fruit.

However, there is more they can do. Dollops of whipped cream and tiny scoops of ice cream or sherbet can be created with the melon ball maker. It is even good for some dropped cookie dough recipes by assuring consistently-sized treats.

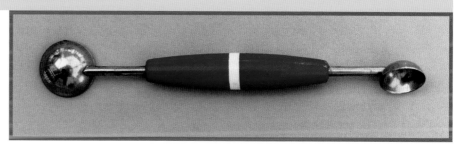

This 7.75" long melon ball maker is marked "EKCO U.S.A." on each ball end. Circa 1930s-1940s. $10.

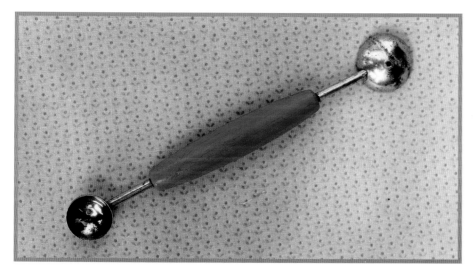

Two differently-sized melon balls can be made with this 7.5" long tool. Circa late 1920-1930s. $10.

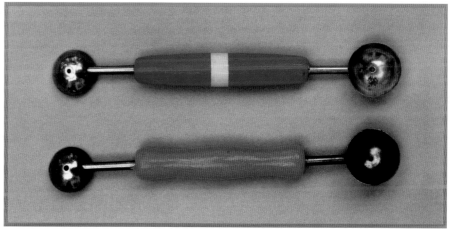

These two 7.25" long melon ball makers are particularly interesting. Few striped red-handled tools have such a wide stripe, and pink-handled tools are very hard to find. Red, Circa 1930s-1940s, $10; pink, Circa 1950s, $15.

 # apkin Holders

One can assume virtually any napkin holder is probably no earlier than the middle of the 1900s because of the lack of counter space. Once a collector has one napkin holder it is unlikely that additional ones will be purchased even though an assortment of sizes, shapes, and styles is available.

Think creatively! Napkin holders can be used to hold note paper, mail, and even an open cookbook.

Marked "MADE IN U.S.A.," this 8.75" long, 5.75" tall metal napkin holder has a simple triangular design. Circa late 1940s. $15.

This 8.25" tall metal napkin holder seems to be made with two trivets. Circa 1950s. $15.

This 6" tall wire frame is designed to hold hand-crocheted pieces that look similar to hot pads. As shown here there is little value. Circa late 1940s-early 1950s. With the hand-made sleeves, $12.

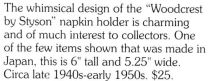

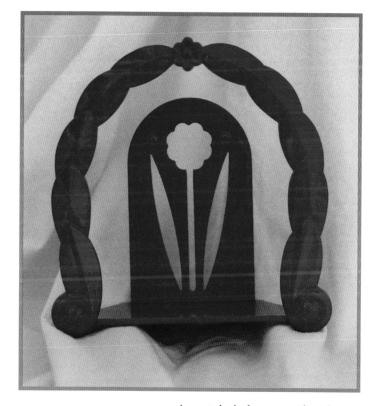

The whimsical design of the "Woodcrest by Styson" napkin holder is charming and of much interest to collectors. One of the few items shown that was made in Japan, this is 6" tall and 5.25" wide. Circa late 1940s-early 1950s. $25.

A great deal of care must be taken with simple plastic napkin holders as they are easily damaged. This holder is marked "MADE IN U.S.A. A 4 PATENT APPLIED FOR." Circa 1950s. $12.

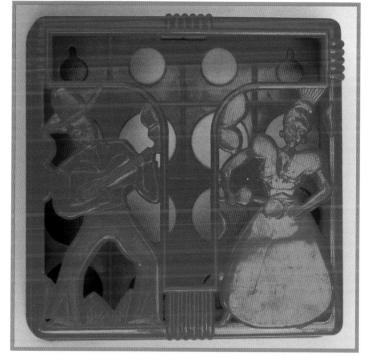

Mexican themes were popular for kitchen décor in the late 1940s and 1950s. Fiesta dinnerware was a part of this craze and an 8" square napkin holder reflected this trend. This plastic holder was designed to sit on a counter or to hang on a wall. Circa late 1940s-1950s. $30.

Openers

Today if you ask someone to describe a kitchen opener most likely you'd hear about an electric can opener. Press the issue and ask for something manual and you might get something similar to the two green-handled tools shown, but without the color or wood… the old squeeze and crank gizmo.

Storing provisions and then getting to the contents of the container in which they were held is nothing new. For centuries man has done this, but our past few decades have left us with an interesting portfolio of human creativity. An array of colors, materials, and designs were used to open jars, bottles, and cans.

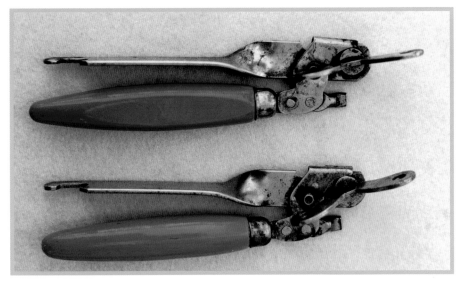

In honor of the squeeze and crank method of opening a can, here are two 6.5" long "MIRACLE CAN OPENER(s) MADE IN UNITED STATES OF AMERICA-PAT. PEND. HOLD IN LEFT HAND-HOOK GEAR UNDER RIM OF CAN-SQUEEZE HANDLES-TURN KEY TO RIGHT." Yes, directions are engraved right onto the metal, as this was such a new and inventive way to access the contents of a can many would have no idea what to do or how to do it. A bottle opener is conveniently located on the end of each. Circa 1930s. $14 each.

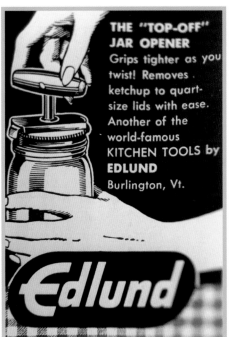

Shown in the April 1957 issue of *Ladies' Home Journal* the TOP-OFF is still a vital tool in American kitchens almost twenty-five years after its introduction.

The "TOP-OFF JAR & BOTTLE SCREW TOP OPENER" was one of many patented openers by Edlund Company, Inc. of Burlington, Vermont. This had a range of 3" to 3.75" with a turn of the handle. The patent is from 1933. Circa 1933. $14.

The Eversharp Can Opener by The Acme Shear Company was offered as a Sunbrite premium in November 1940. This wall-mounted opener was designed to operate with one hand.

Edlund Company, Inc. of Burlington, Vermont manufactured several different can opener designs. This advertisement for the "JUNIOR" was in the March 1948 issue of *Better Homes and Gardens*.

Made in green, yellow, turquoise, and red, the Edlund "JUNIOR" can still be found with the original sticker that provides directions for its operation. Circa late 1940s. $12 with sticker.

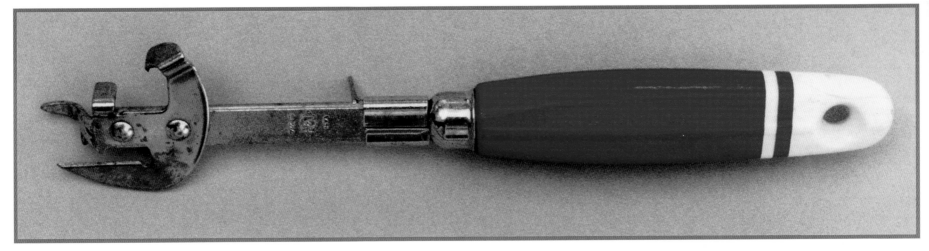

A & J manufactured this 8.75" long opener. Circa 1930s. $14.

This 7" long opener is marked "TOOL STEEL TEMPERED EKCO U.S.A." Circa 1930s. $14.

There is no manufacturer's information on this 6.5" long wooden-handled opener. Circa 1930s. $14.

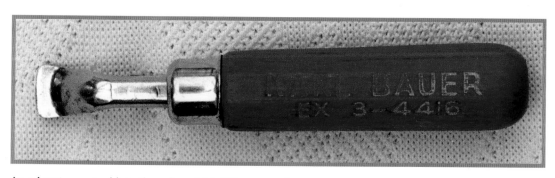

An advertisement adds to the value of this 5" long wooden-handled bottle opener. Circa late 1940s-early 1950s. $14.

The Grip-All Screw Cap Opener states its function right on the metal: "OPENS AND CLOSES ALL SIZES." It is 8" long with a red wooden handle. Circa early 1940s. $20.

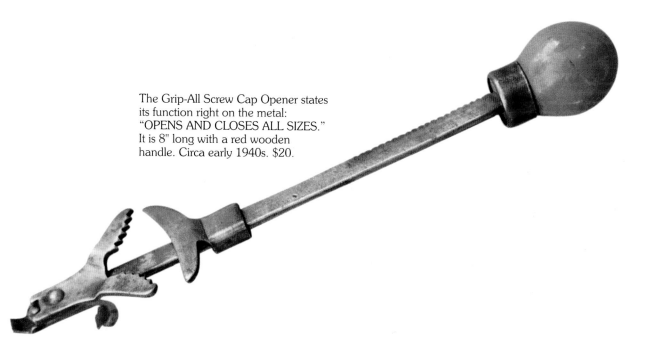

A range of 4.5" to 8.75" would meet most needs with this Cinch Cap Remover by SEECO. It is marked "PAT. PEND. MADE IN U.S.A." Circa 1930s. $20.

Barware has become quite collectible, and this whimsical grouping would delight many. Made from a composition material, the corkscrew is 3.5" long, the bottle opener is almost 4" long, and the cork stopper is 3.5" long. Circa 1930s. $25 each.

Bakelite-handled openers are difficult to find. The corkscrew is 4.5" long with a 3.75" long handle. The wooden-handled bottle opener is almost 4" long. Neither tool has any manufacturer's marking. Circa 1930s. Bakelite, $30; wood, $10.

Yellow Bakelite-handled kitchen tools are much less common than red ones. This 4.75" long bottle opener has no manufacturer's information. Circa 1930s. $30.

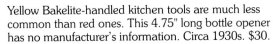

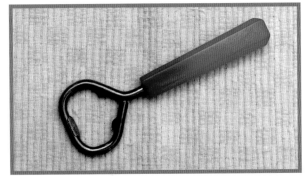

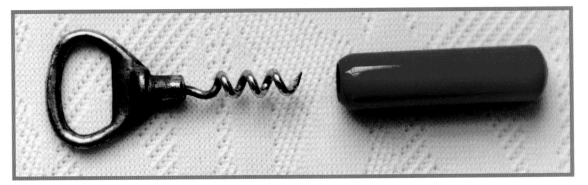

A 2.5" long Bakelite cylinder houses a 3.25" long opener/corkscrew combination. Circa 1930s. $50.

Pie Crimpers

With the demise of baking from scratch, the use of some kitchen tools has waned. Such is the case of the pie crimper, a tool that many often cannot even recognize.

A pie crimper can trim the edge of the top or lid of pie pastry. It can also crimp or pleat the edge while assisting in sealing the top to the bottom pie shell.

Early pie crimpers can be found in wood, metal, and bone. Crimpers from the 1920s-1950s were made primarily with wood or plastic handles and the cutting edge can be metal or plastic. On rare occasions Bakelite pie crimpers can be found.

The designs are varied; collecting pie crimpers could offer a fun challenge and reward the collector with unique kitchen tools.

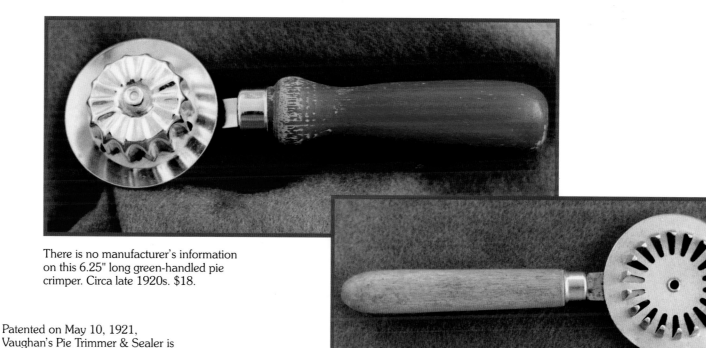

There is no manufacturer's information on this 6.25" long green-handled pie crimper. Circa late 1920s. $18.

Patented on May 10, 1921, Vaughan's Pie Trimmer & Sealer is 6.25" long. The red wooden handle can be no earlier than 1927. Vaughan also produced pie crimpers with Bakelite handles. Circa late 1920s. $18.

Few collectors show interest in plain wooden handles as on this "Corona Quality Pie Trimmer & Sealer." Circa late 1940s. $8.

This 5.25" long plastic-handled pie crimper is marked "PLASMETL MADE IN U.S.A. PATENT PENDING 3." Circa early 1950s. $12.

There is no manufacturer's information on this 5" long plastic pie crimper. Circa 1950s. $10.

Pizza Cutters

One of the most elusive kitchen tools of all is the pizza cutter. In the fifties, "Pizza Pie" as it was called was an exotic treat and home delivery was nonexistent; there was little need of this tool. Now collectors compete to own the few vintage pizza cutters that were made and survived.

Pizza cutters can be found with red wooden handles and with Bakelite handles. Care needs to be taken to verify that the tool being considered for purchase is actually a pizza cutter and not a sewing tool or pie crimper. Look for a single, smooth metal disk with a cutting edge completely around the circumference.

A similar 8.25" long wooden-handled pizza cutter is marked "STAINLESS U.S.A." Circa late 1950s. $25.

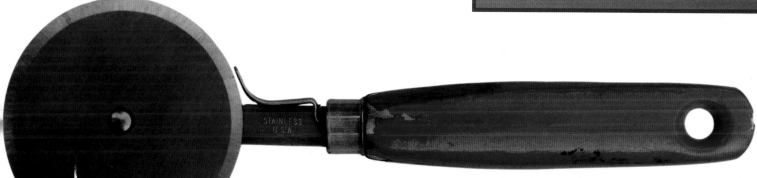

Marked only "STAINLESS U.S.A." this 8.25" long pizza cutter remains in relatively good condition. Circa late 1950s. $25.

Potato Mashers

Another generation was beginning to enjoy the comfort food "smashed potatoes" when along came new dietary theories that say good-bye to the carbohydrates. One might not buy a masher for use, but as an addition to a collection of vintage kitchen tools it cannot be overlooked.

Yellow handles with a single green stripe are hard to find and beginning to get popular. This 9.5" wooden-handled masher has matching kitchen tools that will take some searching to find. Circa 1930s. $12.

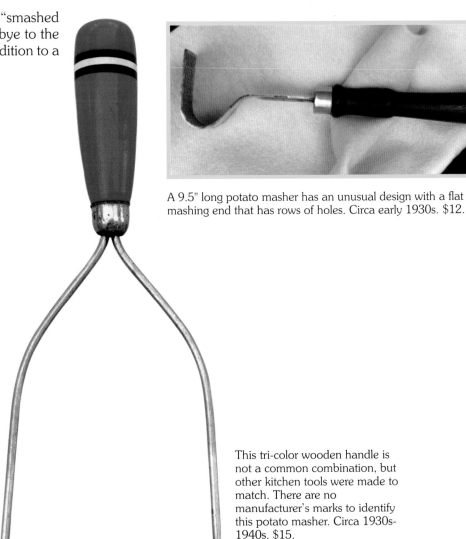

A 9.5" long potato masher has an unusual design with a flat mashing end that has rows of holes. Circa early 1930s. $12.

This tri-color wooden handle is not a common combination, but other kitchen tools were made to match. There are no manufacturer's marks to identify this potato masher. Circa 1930s-1940s. $15.

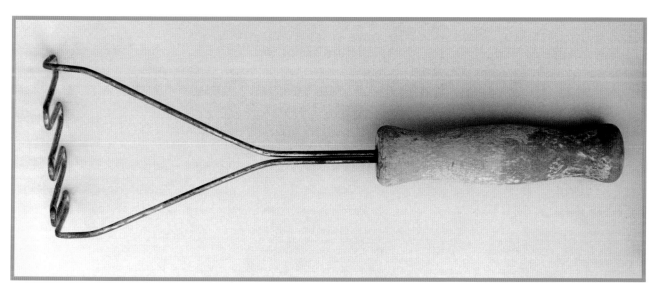

Although collectors of vintage kitchenware would probably not purchase a tool with such a worn handle, crafters might find this a usable element for a project. Circa late 1920s. $3.

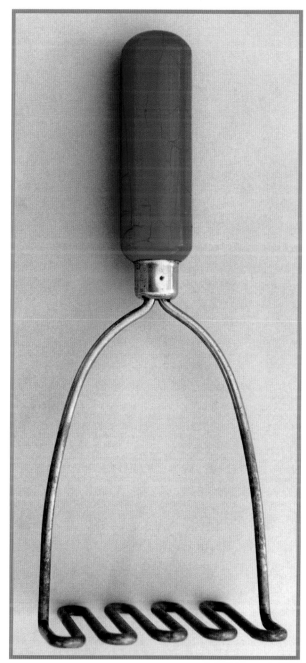

A plain red handle is usually in less demand with collectors than one with stripes of color. Circa 1930s. $8.

115

Scoops

Whether reaching for flour or serving ice cream, scoops are useful, interesting, and popular. Wooden-handled scoops are the most common and can be found with 1/4-, 1/2-, and 1-cup markings. Bakelite-handled scoops are difficult to find and one can expect to pay $50 or more to acquire one. After World War II, plastic kitchen tools became popular, and plastic scoops were produced along with a plethora of other gadgets and tools.

This 7.25" long green-handled scoop is marked "LEVEL FULL 1/4 CUP UTILITY MADE IN U.S.A." Circa late 1920s. $12.

The Latest Cake Secrets copyrighted in 1934 by General Foods Corporation shows a red-handled scoop ready to measure the flour.

A single white stripe adds interest to the handle and augments the value of this 7.5" long scoop marked "A & J LEVEL FULL 1/4 CUP MADE IN UNITED STATES OF AMERICA." Circa 1930s. $15.

Additional color on a wooden handle enhances the value of this "LEVEL FULL 1/4 CUP A & J MADE IN U.S.A." scoop. Circa 1930s-1940s. $15.

Both scoops are marked "A & J LEVEL FULL ...CUP." The small one is 1/4-cup and the large one is 1/2-cup. Plain red handles are not as popular as those with a stripe or two, but the fact that these are scoops still makes them desirable. Circa 1930s. $10 each with wear as shown.

Although not easily found in pristine condition, black-handled kitchen tools are relatively unpopular and thus of lower value than counterparts in other colors. This 7.75" long scoop is marked "LEVEL FULL 1/4 CUP EKCO U.S.A." Circa 1930s. $10.

Red wooden handles are usually less popular when missing a stripe or two. However, any colored wooden-handled ice cream scoop is a rare find. Circa 1930s. $35.

Similar in design to the Bakelite-handled paddle style ice cream scoop, an 8.5" long plastic-handled scoop has no manufacturer's information. Circa late 1940s. $20.

Ice cream scoops prior to 1927 have no color decorating the wooden handles. Collectors of ice cream memorabilia or early kitchenware will appreciate examples from the early 1900s. However, collectors decorating with the 1920s-1950s theme will probably pass on these due to the absence of color. The longer scoop is 11.25" and has a "24" on the thumb lever. The 9.75" scoop is marked "1UDHOP CANADA." Circa early 1920s. $25 each.

Ice cream scoops are available in a variety of configurations. This paddle style is easy to use but hard to find. Shown is a 9" long ice cream scoop with a black Bakelite handle. Circa 1930s-early 1940s. $55.

A two-colored plastic handle is on a scoop marked "LEVEL FULL 1/4 CUP ANDROCK MADE IN U.S.A." The pristine condition of this tool enhances its value. Circa late 1940s-early 1950s. $15.

Lustro-Ware products are favorites among collectors of plastic kitchenware. Finding original packaging only makes a treasure more spectacular. These three scoops were sold for twenty-nine cents, a bargain for "Corrosion proof easy to clean" tools. Circa late 1940s-1950s. $25 as packaged.

The Lustro-Ware "kitchen ensemble" was manufactured by Columbus Products, Inc., Columbus, Ohio. This listing of kitchenware was found on the back panel of a Lustro-Ware package.

119

Although a red-handled ice cream scoop is pictured on the front of this box, the side panel is stamped with "BLACK." This is the #20 Black Model 601 Peerless Machine & Tool Corporation's Bakelite-handled scoop made in Brooklyn, New York. Circa 1930s. $55; add $20 for box.

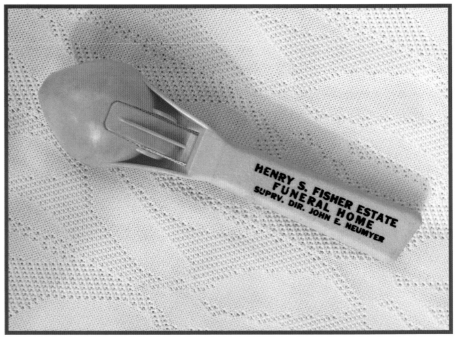

This pink plastic ice cream scoop is from the "Villaware" line of kitchenware manufactured by Federal Housewares of Chicago, Illinois. This 7.5" long scoop is particularly interesting because of the advertisement. Imagine a funeral director passing out ice cream scoops! Circa 1950s. $15 with an ad as shown.

Scrapers

The statement underneath the photograph says it all, "Use good tools to insure baking success." From the General Foods Corporation's cookbook *All About Home Baking* copyrighted in 1936, one can see what the "good tools" were, and among them is a scraper.

Finding a scraper is difficult, finding one in excellent condition is almost impossible. As a tool that was used few survived, and the rubber from which they were made tended to dry out, crack, and fall apart.

Use good tools to insure baking success

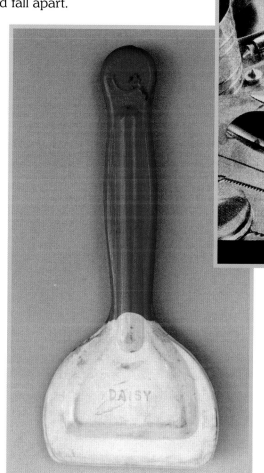

A 1933 patent protects the Daisy scraper. The other side of this is marked "SCHACHT RUBBER MFG CO. HUNTINGTON INDI- ANA." A scraper in this like-new condition is very hard to find. Circa 1930s. $15.

Shown is another Daisy scraper in good condition. Exposure to either heat or sunlight has caused the red handle to darken and the rubber to stiffen. Circa 1930s. $12.

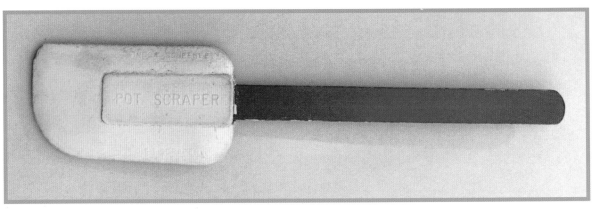

This style was so successful it is still being manufactured. Vintage tools have a rubber head often marked "POT SCRAPER" and a wooden handle. New scrapers are plastic. Circa late 1930s-1940s. $15.

A green Daisy scraper is pictured in this image from *Baker's Famous Chocolate Recipes* copyrighted in 1936 by General Foods Corporation.

The 10.5" long Kitchen King has a "BOWL AND PLATE SCRAPER" and a metal "PAN SCRAPER." Although the rubber has deteriorated, this is such a unique tool most collectors would be thrilled to own it. Circa 1930s. $30.

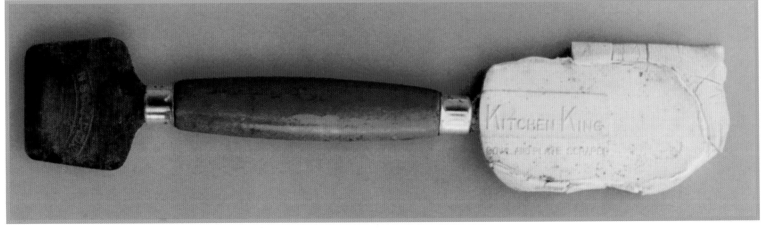

Sharpeners

In our disposable society, the function of a sharpening tool is lost on many collectors. Generations past used and reused everything; possessions were important, and all things had value. A knife was not something to use and discard after the blade dulled. Tools existed to give a dull blade new life and many more years of function. If given the opportunity to look through the tools and gadgets in a kitchen fifty years ago, one would see an assortment of misshapen knife blades indicating they had been sharpened multiple times.

There are basically two types of sharpeners from the period of the 1920s-1950s. The first style is carborundum sharpeners that had a gritty, stone-like end upon which a dull knife blade would be drawn. The second variety is sharpeners that have two or more disks through which a blade would be pulled.

Few collectors purchase sharpeners for actual use even though they are effective tools that achieve what they are designed to do. However, sharpening a blade will slowly wear it away, and this is something to consider prior to working on a vintage knife blade.

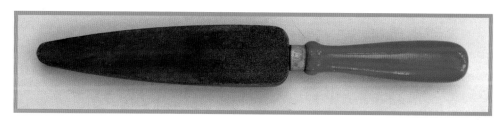

Simply marked "CARBORUNDUM," this 10.25" long sharpener would be a wonderful addition to a red-handled kitchen tool collection. Circa 1930s. $18.

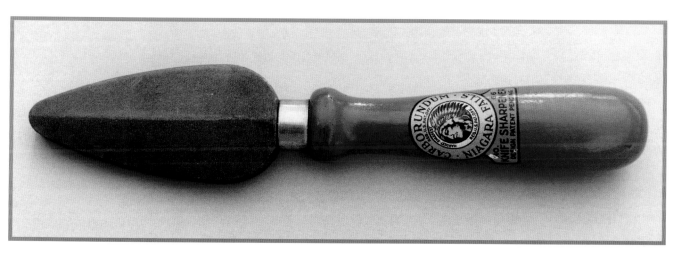

This 7.25" long sharpener retains its original sticker that reads "CARBORUNDUM NIAGARA FALLS NO. 66 KNIFE SHARPENER DESIGN PATENT PENDING." Circa 1930s. $25.

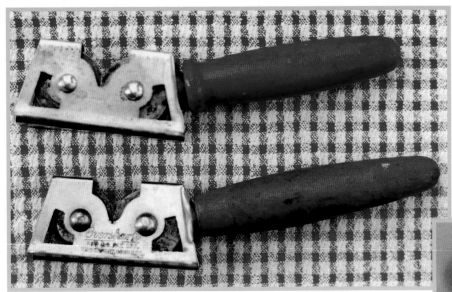

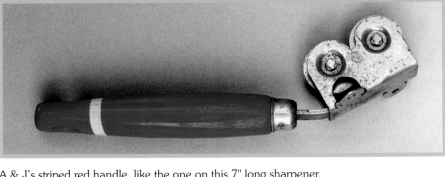

A & J's striped red handle, like the one on this 7" long sharpener, is one of the most popular with collectors. Circa 1930s. $10.

Both Eversharp tools are marked "REG.U.S.PAT.OFF.BRIDGEPORT, CONN.U.S.A." One is 5.5" long and the other is 5" long. Circa 1930s. $10.

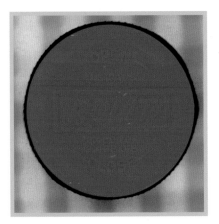

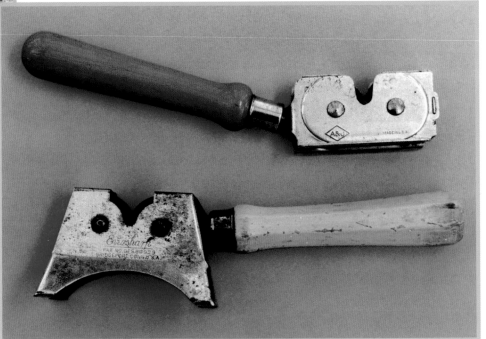

The "ROLIT" sharpener is designed with a carborundum disk in the center. A knife blade is rolled across the side of the disk creating the rolling motion for which the sharpener is named. This Rolit has patents from 1949 and 1950. Circa 1950. $14.

A & J manufactured the 6.75" long green-handled sharpener. The yellow-handled sharpener is another example of an Eversharp tool. Although in poor condition, yellow-handled sharpeners are quite rare so this still has value. Circa 1930s. $15 each.

A & J's striped handles as on this 6.75" long sharpener are among the most popular with collectors. Circa 1930s. $18.

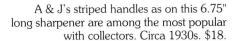

Sifters

The mechanisms that operate a sifter have changed little in the twentieth century. There are several configurations, and all are effective.

One of the earliest sifter designs operates by squeezing the handle to activate screens that sift.

Shaking the apparatus back and forth in a sideways motion activated another sifter mechanism. Foley produced these in several sizes including a 2-cup size that allowed the sifter to fit in the flour bin of a Hoosier-Style kitchen cabinet.

A "SIFT-CHINE" sifter was used in creating cookies in an advertisement from the December 1939 issue of the *Ladies' Home Journal*.

The "SIFT-CHINE" was such a successful device it is still offered for only $1.65 in the February 1952 issue of the *Ladies' Home Journal*. It was available with yellow, red, or green bands.

The last sifter mechanism is one that cranks with a rotating knob. Most American-made sifters had the crank handle on the side and most Canadian-made sifters had a crank handle at the top. There are exceptions as shown with the first two sifters.

The Foley sifter shown in an offer from April 1941 was a free gift with the purchase of certain Proctor & Gamble products.

The single most popular sifter is this one by Androck. Also a "HAND-i-SIFT" sifter, there is a 1952 patent date on it. Circa 1950s. $70.

Canisters, a bread box, and more were manufactured with the same motif as shown on this unmarked triple sifter that originally sold for $1.69. Circa 1940s. $30.

Two of the most popular and difficult-to-find metal kitchenware designs are the cherry and strawberry motifs shown on these sifters. The strawberry sifter is marked "HAND-i-SIFT MADE IN US of A." Circa 1940s. $45 each.

The "BROMWELL'S MEASURING SIFTER GUARANTEED" has increments from two cups to five cups. Most collectors prefer colorfully decorated sifters. Bromwell is still manufacturing sifters and this causes some confusion for collectors. Circa 1930s. $20.

Although this has a crank handle at the top, this is marked "MADE IN USA." The red handle, knob, and bands make this an attractive addition to any red and white kitchen. Circa 1930s. $40.

The original forty-five cent price remains on an apple sifter with a crank mechanism. There is no manufacturer's information on this sifter, but the apple motif was a Deco Ware design. These are being reproduced! New sifters have a plastic knob rather than a wooden one. Circa 1930s. $30.

Spatulas

Server, flipper, or spatula… whatever the name, there is no other kitchen tool that can do what these handy tools do. They can loosen food from a hot surface, lift a delicate food item, turn over a flimsy food, and serve that which has been prepared.

The array of spatulas is almost unending. Collectors usually consider two features when making a purchase: handle and design. A decision to make a purchase can be made based on the color(s) of the handle, the uniqueness of the handle, and the distinctiveness of the metal design. Of course, condition is quite important.

Although the handles are not particularly exciting, the interesting metal design makes these desirable. The 12.75" long green-handled spatula is unmarked. The 13.75" long black-handled spatula is marked "MIRRO The Finest Aluminum MADE IN U.S.A. TRADEMARK REGISTERED." Circa early 1930s. Green, $14; black, $8.

An expandable spatula is shown in the September 1939 issue of *The American Home*. These are usually found with red handles and are a favorite with collectors. Circa late 1930s-early 1940s. $20.

The 13" spatula is marked "A & J MADE IN U.S.A." Circa 1950s. $12.

Nothing says "Fifties" more than a kitchen with lots of yellow. A spatula hangs with other tools in a scene pictured in the October 1957 issue of *Ladies' Home Journal.*

The Scrapers section also shows Daisy products that are virtually the same as these 9.25" long spatulas except for the manufacturer's marking: "DAISY KITCHEN SPATULA SCHACHT RUBBR MFG. COMPANY HUNTINGTON, INDIANA. Circa 1930s. $15 each.

Breakfast need not be monotonous

A hard-to-find blue-handled spatula is poised to serve some pancakes in the colorful breakfast scene from the January 1945 issue of *The American Home.*

This 13.75" long tri-color wooden-handle is not a common combination, but other kitchen tools were made to match. It is marked "ANDROCK MADE IN UNITED STATES OF AMERICA" and "CHROME PLATE." Circa 1930s-1940s. $15.

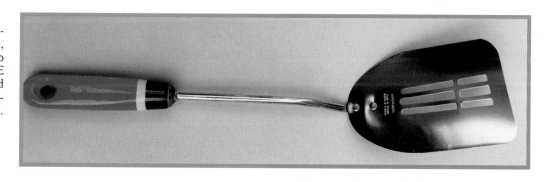

Spoon Holders

The spoon holders or spoon rests shown here are all plastic. Care needs to be taken as they are likely to burn, scorch, or melt if exposed to a high enough temperature. Because of the susceptibility of damage caused by heat many plastic spoon holders, as well as coasters, are marked "do not use for ash tray."

Businesses often advertised on plastic spoon holders, and local interest by collectors would result in a higher value within a geographic area.

Plastic chef kitchenware is in high demand, and this 6" long turquoise spoon holder is a great color with the addition of an advertisement. Circa 1950s. $15.

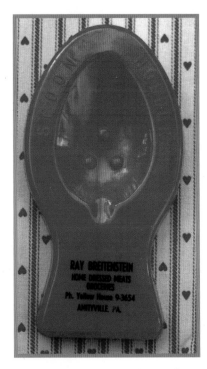

A Pennsylvania grocer advertised on a 5.25" long spoon holder. Circa 1950s. $10.

The Fuller Brush Company produced this 5.25" long pear-shaped spoon holder. Circa 1950s. $8.

Although orange is a color often overlooked by collectors of vintage kitchenware, this 6.5" tall chef double spoon holder deserves attention and consideration for purchase. Circa 1950s. $12.

${\cal S}$poons

Spoons are found in the same handle colors and styles as most other cooking tools such as spatulas, forks, and strainers. Spoons are one of the most versatile of all kitchen tools as they are used in baking, cooking, and serving.

An advertisement for EKCO red-handled tools was in the June 6, 1955 issue of *Life Magazine.* The slotted spoon was actually called a "mixing spoon" and the small solid-bowled spoon was called a "basting spoon." A four-piece set was only eighty-eight cents or twenty-two cents apiece!

The article from the July 1949 issue of *The American Home* is entitled "Where to begin…" and three of the thirteen items are spoons: #2 "Wooden spoons, fine for stirring as they are poor conductors of heat," #11 "Slotted spoon with multiple uses," #13 "Sturdy measuring spoons made of aluminum, a must for accurate seasoning."

Where to begin...

Preserving summer's bounty is easier if you take stock of equipment

before beginning . . . pictorial check list to expedite procedure, influence results

EDITH RAMSAY

TO CAN OR TO FREEZE: Perhaps this is your first year of housekeeping, and you want to do yourself proud. Or maybe you have been an apartment dweller in the past, and now you have a kitchen large enough to include a pantry or freezer. In either case, it will be helpful to look over what you have in the way of preserving equipment. Then check our pictures for additional pieces to simplify the summer's work before you.

Follow the latest instructions from an authoritative source for methods of preparing and processing foods. Make certain all equipment is in good working condition and follow manufacturer's instructions for using.

If you are a beginner, wise buying will pay dividends. There are utensils you use every day which are needed for your preserving program. They are not used specifically in any one type of preserving, so we have made a separate grouping of them.

1. Large colander for washing fruits and vegetables, also steaming. This one fits into its own kettle.

2. Wooden spoons, fine for stirring as they are poor conductors of heat.

3. Household scales save time and frequent guesswork.

4. Enamel kettle, because of non-staining properties, is perfect for pickles, relishes, spiced fruits.

5. Layer cake tin filled with hot water used to place jars in while filling. Also used in freezing, placed under dripping wire basket full of scalded vegetables.

6. Bowls of many sizes are another necessity.

7. Liquid and dry measures of heat-resistant glass can be used for measuring hot as well as cold liquids and foods.

8. Nested measuring cups from one-quarter cup to one cup.

9. Cutting board for slicing and chopping food.

10. French knife used for chopping.

11. Slotted spoon with multiple uses.

12. Paring knives of two sizes means having the right tool for the job.

13. Sturdy measuring spoons of aluminum, a must for accurate seasoning.

PLEASE TURN TO PAGE 62

The June 1948 issue of *Ladies' Home Journal* advertised EKCOLINE tools for the bride that were packaged in the "gay and graceful cylinder." This handle style was called "WinGrip," a semi-triangular design thought to provide comfort with a secure fit. Two spoons are part of the largest set.

This tri-color wooden-handle is not a common combination, but other kitchen tools were made to match. This 11.75" long spoon is marked "ANDROCK MADE IN UNITED STATES OF AMERICA" and "CHROME PLATE." Circa 1930s-1940s. $15.

Sunbeam Bread is advertised on a 5.25" long measuring spoon. The side showing measures one tablespoon and one teaspoon; the other side measures 1/2 teaspoon and 1/4 teaspoon. Circa 1950s. $10.

This 12.25" long wooden-handled slotted spoon is marked "ANDROCK." Circa 1930s. $12.

Both spoons are marked "A & J EKCO U.S.A." which is a manufacturing mark that precedes the EKCO advertisement. Circa 1930s-1940s. $12 each.

A fine mesh assists both straining and mixing with this unique 11" long black-handled spoon. Circa 1930s. $15.

Spreaders

The primary function of a spreader is to spread icing. They do come in handy assisting in other kitchen tasks such as loosening cake or muffins from baking tins, and serving brownies, lasagna, and even fish.

Most companies created sets of kitchen tools that could be purchased in groups or singly, but the goal was to have as many as possible of the newest style in every American home. The examples shown have handles that have been seen in preceding sections of this book and would have been part of a manufacturer's latest offerings.

Neither of these spreaders have any manufacturer's information. The solid red-handled spreader is 11" long and the tri-colored-handled spreader is 11.75" long. Circa 1930s-1940s. Plain red, $10; tri-colored, $14.

The 12.25" long spreader has no manufacturer's markings, but a whip with the same handle is marked A & J. Circa 1950s. $12.

This tri-color wooden-handle is not a common combination, but other kitchen tools were made to match. There are no manufacturer's marks to identify this 11.25" long spreader, but a spatula pictured in this book is marked with the Androck name. Circa 1930s-1940s. $15.

Strainers

Found in a huge assortment of diameters from tiny to large, strainers are an extremely useful kitchen tool. Most strainers, like forks, spatulas, and other tools, are part of a set.

Condition of the mesh is essential as strainers with rust should not be used. To avoid denting or crushing the mesh it is recommended that the strainer be hung rather than placed in a drawer. Our mothers and grand-mothers would have displayed their colorfully-handled tools with pride. Most strainers have a loop or two that assist in hanging a strainer, but the primary purpose of the loops was to allow the strainer to rest on a pot or bowl.

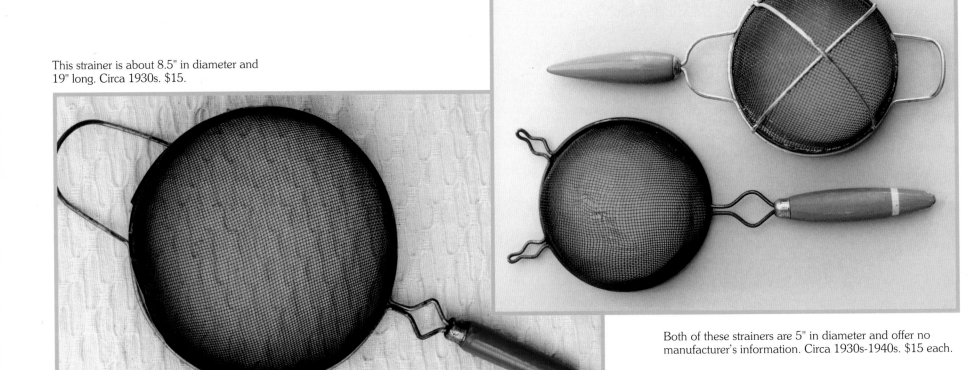

This strainer is about 8.5" in diameter and 19" long. Circa 1930s. $15.

Both of these strainers are 5" in diameter and offer no manufacturer's information. Circa 1930s-1940s. $15 each.

The fine mesh and mere 3.25" diameter of this strainer makes it perfect for tea. Circa 1930s-1940s. $15 each.

An original twenty-nine cent price tag enhances the value of a strainer with a 3.25" diameter. Circa 1930s. $18 with sticker as shown.

A hole in the handle allows one to hang 6.25" diameter strainer. Many solid red-handled tools do not have a hole. Circa 1930s. $12.

This 8.25" diameter strainer is marked "ANDROCK MADE IN U.S.A." Circa 1930s. $12.

135

The mesh of this 3.25" diameter strainer is more coarse than most. This is marked "ANDROCK PAT. NO. 1874410 MADE IN U.S.A. 3 1/4 IN. 8 MESH." The patent date is from 1932. Circa 1932. $14.

A 1935 patent date is on a 5" diameter strainer marked "AJAX HEAVY DUTY STRAINER MADE IN U.S.AMERICA PAT. No. 2006566." Circa 1935. $14.

This yellow-handled strainer has a diameter of 2.75" and the same patent number as the last red-handled Androck strainer pictured previously. This is marked "ANDROCK PAT. NO. 1874410 MADE IN U.S.A." Yellow-handled strainers are difficult to find. Circa 1930s. $18.

This 2.5" diameter strainer is marked "ANDROCK MADE IN U.S.A." A tri-colored wooden handle is difficult to find in any condition. Circa 1930s-1940s. $14.

Pink-handled kitchen tools are extremely rare and handles in the wonderful condition shown here are a treasure. The strainers are 3.25" and 5" in diameter. Circa 1950s. $14 each.

The same company that produced the two pink-handled strainers probably manufactured this 3.25" diameter strainer in turquoise. Circa 1950s. $14.

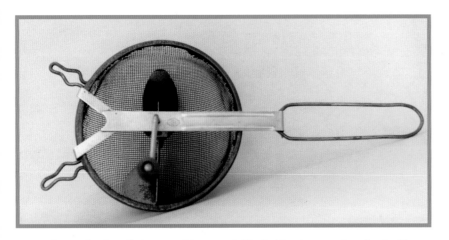

A wooden handle is moved in a crank-like fashion to operate a food mill that snaps onto a 6.25" diameter strainer. This is marked "A & J MADE IN UNITED STATES OF AMERICA." Circa late 1920s. $15.

The addition of a mechanical apparatus turns a strainer into a food mill. This configuration functions by squeezing the two metal pieces causing two pieces that are positioned in the center of the mesh to sweep back and forth. Circa 1930s. $20.

It is unusual to find fine mesh on a strainer as large as this 5" diameter example. This plastic-handled strainer is marked "PLASMETL REG. TRADE MARK U.S. PATENTS NO. 2391215 AND FOREIGN PATS. MADE IN U.S.A. 2." Circa 1950s. $15.

This 2.5" diameter strainer is marked "ANDROCK MADE IN U.S.A." Circa late 1940s-1950s. $14.

Syrup Pitchers

Syrup pitchers were designed to dispense syrup without a single drip. They may not have always stood up to their guarantee, but they did stand up to the test of time as decades later collectors continue to love syrup pitchers.

Most of the time the glass bases of syrup pitchers are crystal (clear) and may be marked by the company that produced them. The lids are usually metal, metal and Bakelite, metal and plastic, or plastic.

Sometimes syrup pitchers were purchased, sometimes they were acquired as a premium or gift, and sometimes they held a consumable product. Once the product was used the homemaker was left with a "free" dispenser.

Large dispensers with a similar design as those that follow were batter pitchers, and often there was one of each in the kitchen. Batter could be neatly poured into a griddle or pan for cooking while the syrup pitcher waited at the table with hungry family members.

The base is marked "E1269" and the metal and Bakelite lid is marked "PAT'D U.S.A." For only fifty cents and a proof of purchase from Karo Syrup a homemaker could get the 6.5" tall "Karo Syrup Pitcher." Circa 1939-1940. $40.

Gift ideas are presented in the May 1940 issue of *The American Home*. The syrup and batter pitchers are by Universal Potteries, Incorporated while the ones presented next are glass. However, the handles of the Universal pitchers are Bakelite "Bullets" by Androck and some of the glass syrups that follow have this same handle design.

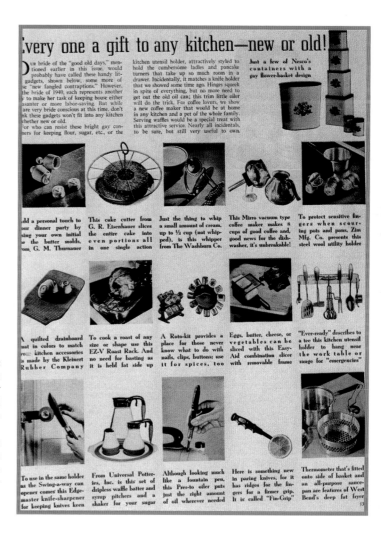

139

The taller syrup dispenser is marked "Dripcut 214 MADE IN U.S.A." The smaller pitcher has a plastic and metal lid. Without color or interesting glass these would have little interest to most collectors. Circa 1950s. $8 each.

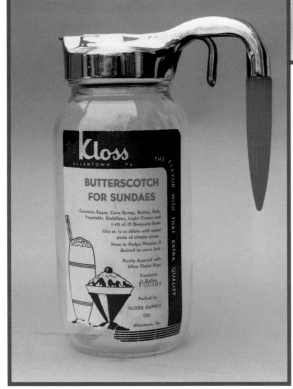

At 8" in height this container originally held a quart of butterscotch. The base was produced by Hazel-Atlas, and the lid was manufactured by Federal Tool Corporation of Chicago. The lid has a patent from 1938. Circa 1938. $50 with label, $40 without.

Both of the dispensers have Bakelite handles. The green-handled lid is marked "3A Dripcut MADE IN U.S.A." and is 5.5" tall. The gold-handled lid is marked "FEDERAL HOUSEWARES FEDCO CORPORATION CHICAGO 45 ILLINOIS 6" with a patent date from 1932 and is 5" tall. Circa 1930s. $25 each.

The plain syrup is marked "DES. PAT. PENDING MEDC PROD. N.Y.4." and the floral-decorated syrup is marked "Dripcut MADE IN U.S.A." Both are about 6" tall and have plastic lids with metal covers over the spout. Circa 1940s-early 1950s. Plain, $18; decorated, $35.

There are no markings on an 8.5" tall frosted glass pitcher that features hand painted flowers. Circa 1950s. $30.

The bulbous glass bases of the 5.75" tall and 4.5" tall pitchers have no manufacturer's information. The red lid is marked "Dripcut" so one can assume the green lid is also a Dripcut product. Circa 1940s-early 1950s. $18 each.

Both lids have the same marking: "DO NOT BOIL PAT. NO. 2,276,917 USE WARM WATER FOR CLEANING FEDERAL TOOL CORP. CHICAGO, ILL." The patent date for the lid mechanism is from 1943 but these were probably made after the conclusion of World War II. Circa 1943-early 1950s. $15 each.

Collectors usually prefer syrup dispensers that have a metal cover to the spout; lids that are totally plastic are often overlooked as the mechanism seems poorly made in comparison. These 5.25" pitchers overcome the all-plastic dilemma as the bases retain original stickers. The blue syrup pitcher's label reads "STOP DRIP HOLLYWOOD." The yellow pitcher is another "FEDERAL No Drip SERVER" by Federal Tool Corporation. Circa 1950s. $25 each.

The blue and white syrup pitcher has a lid marked "PAL DISPENSER PAT. 2,187,927 NO DRIP." This is a 1940 patent date. The base is unmarked. The lid with the rare light blue handle is marked "Dripcut" and the base is marked "2B Dripcut 112 Made in U.S.A." Circa 1940-1950s. Blue and white, $25; light blue, $20.

The lid of this 5" tall syrup pitcher is simply marked "JAPAN." The base is fired-on in orange, a color often overlooked by most collectors. Circa late 1940s-early 1950s. $35.

Whips

Some of the most interestingly designed kitchen tools are whips. They can be found in a number of wire and flat metal configurations. The handles often match handles pictured throughout these pages, with one exception: there is one whip pictured that is a true one-of-a-kind, at least so far!

Few contemporary cooks use a whip, but for inclusion with a collection of vintage kitchen collectibles it is a necessary addition to the gadget line-up. Whip up some excitement in your display with one of these fun tools!

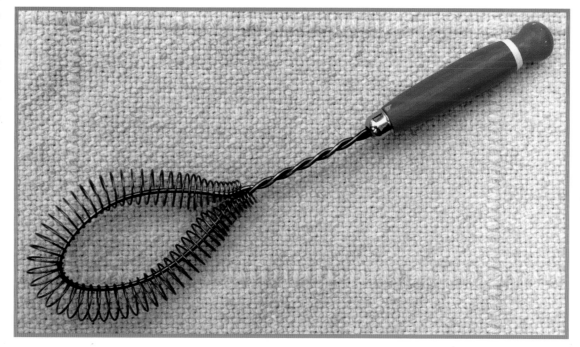

This 12.5" whip has no manufacturer's marks. Circa 1930s. $18.

This 12.5" long A & J whip has a blue and white handle with a metal design that is hard to find. Circa 1930s. $18.

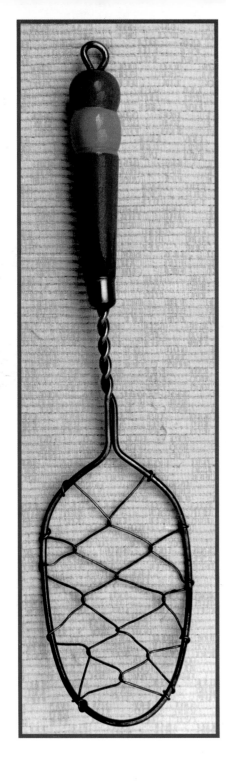

The tool itself says it all: "Kitchamajig STRAINS DRAINS BEATS BLENDS WHIPS MIXES." This 12.25" long A & J tool was made in America. Early 1930s. $10.

The handle configuration of an 11.25" long whip is quite rare. Circa 1930s. $35.

There are no manufacturer's marks on this 12" long two-colored whip. Circa 1930s. $25.